780

With Set Works for examinations from June 2012 to January 2014

AS Music
Study Guide

OCR

Veronica Jamset, Susan Wynne Roberts and Huw Ellis-Williams

R· RHINEGOLD EDUCATION

www.rhinegoldeducation.co.uk

Music Study Guides

GCSE, AS and A2 Music Study Guides (AQA, Edexcel and OCR)
GCSE, AS and A2 Music Listening Tests (AQA, Edexcel and OCR)
AS/A2 Music Technology Study Guide (Edexcel)
AS/A2 Music Technology Listening Tests (Edexcel)
Revision Guides for GCSE (AQA, Edexcel and OCR), AS and A2 Music (Edexcel)

Also available from Rhinegold Education

Key Stage 3 Listening Tests: Book 1 and Book 2
AS and A2 Music Harmony Workbooks
GCSE and AS Music Composition Workbooks
GCSE and AS Music Literacy Workbooks
Romanticism in Focus, Baroque Music in Focus, Film Music in Focus, Modernism in Focus,
The Immaculate Collection in Focus, *Who's Next* in Focus, *Batman* in Focus, *Goldfinger* in Focus, Musicals in Focus
Music Technology from Scratch
Dictionary of Music in Sound

First published 2011 in Great Britain by
Rhinegold Education
14–15 Berners Street
London W1T 3LJ
www.rhinegoldeducation.co.uk

You should always check the current requirement of the examination, since these
may change. Copies of the OCR Specification can be downloaded from the OCR website at www.ocr.org.uk
or may be purchased from OCR Publications, PO Box 5050, Annesley, Nottingham NG15 0DL
Telephone: 0870 770 6622 Email: publications@ocr.org.uk

OCR AS Music Study Guide 4th edition
Order No. RHG205
ISBN 978-1-78038-066-7

Exclusive Distributors:
Music Sales Ltd
Distribution Centre, Newmarket Road
Bury St Edmunds, Suffolk IP33 3YB, UK
Printed in the EU

Contents

(*) The first three jazz recordings in this list are set for examinations from June 2011 until January 2013 while the remaining three are set for examinations from June 2013 onwards.

The details of the specification are believed to be correct at the time of going to press, but you and your teachers should always check current requirements for the examination with OCR since these may change. The music specification is available at www.ocr.org.uk.

The authors

Veronica Jamset taught music in primary and secondary schools in both the state and private sectors in the West Midlands before taking up her first post in Higher Education as a teacher trainer. She worked in two colleges in Birmingham and then moved to St Mary's College at Strawberry Hill in Twickenham, where she became principal lecturer in music and director of in-service and continuing education. Veronica also has considerable experience in adult education. She has been an examiner at various levels since 1990 and, until 2000, was chief examiner for OCR's AS and A-level music syllabuses. She was a member of the team that drafted OCR's current AS/A2 music specification and continues to work as an examiner, reviser and syllabus developer.

Susan Wynne Roberts holds a Master's degree in Composing, Analysis and Criticism from the University of Surrey. She has taught music in a wide range of schools, and for some 16 years has been a senior examiner and moderator for A-level composing, developing well-received materials and schemes of work for A-level teachers. She was part of the team that wrote the current specification for OCR. Sue is an enthusiastic advocate of 20th-century and contemporary music, her interest in the way composers learn to compose taking her as far afield as Boston and Athens. She now teaches music at Greenhead College, Huddersfield.

Huw Ellis-Williams was brought up in Bangor and studied in Oxford and Exeter. A pianist, organist and part-time composer, he teaches at a comprehensive school in north Wales where he is head of sixth form. Huw has a particular interest in instrumental music of the early 20th century, and in music for theatre and film. He is an examiner for OCR. He has contributed to *Classroom Music* and is co-author of the Rhinegold *OCR A2 Music Study Guide*.

Introduction

Course overview

There are three units in the AS music examination for OCR:

➢ Performing Music 1
  (worth 40% of the total AS mark)

➢ Composing 1
  (worth 30% of the total AS mark)

➢ Introduction to Historical Study in Music (sometimes called the 'listening paper', worth 30% of the total AS mark).

OCR stands for 'Oxford, Cambridge and Royal Society of Arts'. It is the organisation that decides what you have to do in each part of this exam, supervises the marking, and awards grades and certificates.

The performing and composing units can only be taken in the summer exam session each year, but the listening paper is set twice a year, in January and June. Most students opt for the June session, since this has the advantage that if you don't do as well as you had hoped it is possible to resit the unit in the following January. Some schools or colleges may let you take the paper early, in the January of your examination year, but if you then want to retake it in June to see if you can improve your mark, you may have to study a new group of set works (see page 70).

Performing

An examiner will come to your centre to hear your performance and discuss it with you. This will happen sometime during the second half of the spring term (March/April) or the beginning of the summer term – you will be told the precise date in advance.

Composing

Your teacher will assess your composing throughout the course and send an overall mark to OCR with samples of your work (which you will probably choose together). This usually happens early in the summer term. OCR's moderator checks through the work to make sure that all the assessment criteria have been met and that standards are being maintained. If the moderator does not agree with your teacher's assessments (if they're too generous or too harsh) the mark can be changed (up or down). This ensures that your mark is in line with national standards.

Introduction to Historical Study in Music

You will sit a two-hour written paper for which you will be given an individual copy of a CD to listen to on your personal stereo in the exam room. Some of the extracts will be from music that you are not expected to have heard before, but others will be from the set works you have studied. The questions will assume that you are *thoroughly familiar* with *all* of the set works. Make sure at the beginning of the course that you know exactly which six pieces you must study – they are listed on page 70.

AS Music is a qualification in its own right. Perhaps you are taking it because you enjoy music and want to broaden your course beyond the subjects that you are planning to take forward to A2. If you work steadily on all three units you will not find it a burden at the end of the course. Performing is usually out of the way by Easter, your composing portfolio will have been submitted at the very beginning of the summer term, and the written examination will not require a lot of last-minute cramming if you have got to know all the music early in your course.

AS is also the first stage of the complete A level in Music: if you intend to go on to A2 you will find that everything you have done at AS has provided you with a firm foundation for the next stage. The A2 units have similar titles and are examined in similar ways.

How this guide will help you

Each unit has a separate chapter that tells you precisely what OCR expects you to do. We have set out all the content in detail and have given you advice on how to prepare.

Although the three units are assessed separately, a common thread runs through them all. This comes from two **areas of study**:

> **Tonality** is about a particular aspect of the language of music and will play an important part in your work for the first half of the composing unit

> **The Expressive Use of Instrumental Techniques** is about how to use instruments effectively, particularly in different combinations, and will be the focus of your work for the second half of the composing unit.

Many of the questions in the listening paper will focus on both of these areas of study. 'The Expressive Use of Instrumental Techniques' is also relevant to Performing Music 1, particularly if you intend to offer an ensemble or composition in Section C.

The chapters on each unit point out clearly how these two areas of study are involved but there is also a short chapter (starting on page 17) which explains them both. Don't be put off the first time you read this chapter if you don't see immediately how it applies to the music you know best. If you come back to it towards the end of your course you will find that you have learned to understand the chapter through *applying* the various points it contains.

Exercises and practice questions

Throughout this book there are short exercises that have been designed to help you understand how what you have read applies to the music you are studying. At the end of each section on the set works there is a group of practice questions. These are not intended to be mini-exam papers but they will give you practice in answering the sorts of question that are often asked in the listening paper. Working through them will also help you to form ways of thinking that will stand you in good stead in the examination.

How you can help yourself

Preparing for the performing unit obviously requires regular practice; exercises for the composing unit must be done throughout the course, not all in the last couple of weeks; and learning about the set works for the listening paper will need plenty of time for you to get to know all six pieces really well. So, you need to plan your time – what you will do each week – and draw up a timetable that shows how and when you will complete all the different parts of your work.

But your AS music course is not a set of unrelated hoops that you must keep jumping through. Although each bit has to be examined separately, all your musical activities support one another:

➤ Being a performer will help you to understand composing and listening

➤ Being a composer will help you to understand performing and listening

➤ Being a perceptive listener will help you to understand your own performing and composing better.

When you do any of these things you are being a *musician* and you will gradually discover, as you work through this book, that everything you learn about music is related:

➤ A detail of how a trumpeter plays in a jazz piece might set you thinking about how trumpets were played in much earlier music, or might give you an idea for your own composing or improvising

➤ Thinking about the structure of one of the pieces you are going to play in your recital will help you shape the music more convincingly and give you extra practice in analysing harmony and form

➤ Working out which notes are harmony notes in a melody for your Section A composing coursework will help you to phrase your own performances intelligently and will prepare you for Section A of the listening paper

➤ Listening to a range of music will help you show an awareness of style and conventions in your own performing.

Because the requirements for Section A of your composing coursework and Section B of the listening paper are fairly precise, we have been able to explain these in plenty of detail to help everyone. But *you* choose all the music you will perform and *you* decide what style of piece to compose for Section B of the composing unit. We can give you quite a lot of general guidance about these and your teachers will give you a great deal of help and encouragement, but the final decisions are yours.

The more you try to make connections for yourself between the different elements of your course, the wiser your decisions will be. If you aim to be a rounded musician who experiences music as a whole, the sooner all the separate elements will fall into place.

Performing

An examiner will come to your school or college to listen to you and discuss your performance with you. The whole performing exam will usually take about 20 minutes.

Section A: Recital (60 marks)

First, you perform a short programme of pieces in which you must be the *soloist*. If you play an instrument which is normally accompanied, like the clarinet, or if you are a singer, then you will need an accompanist. The choice of music is up to you, but two or three contrasting pieces should be enough to give you scope to demonstrate a range of skills and show that you understand different styles.

Your programme should not last more than eight minutes. You do not have to perform for that length of time but if your programme is very short it is unlikely that it will let you show yourself off to best advantage.

Section B: Discussion (20 marks)

After you have played or sung, the examiner will discuss your performance with you. This will not take longer than about five minutes.

Section C: Extended performing (40 marks)

In this part of the examination you have to perform *in a different way from Section A*. You must choose one of the following:

1. Performing a short programme (no more than four minutes long) on a *different* instrument (or voice).

2. Performing in an ensemble or duet. If you play a chordal instrument, such as the piano or guitar, you can choose to perform as an accompanist for this option. Again, a short programme of no more than four minutes in length, is required. Note that:

    ➤ If you had an accompanist in Section A, you cannot do so again for this section and claim that you are now a 'duet' – the examiner needs to hear what *else* you can do

    ➤ The examiner will need to be able to hear your own contribution to the ensemble, so activities such as singing in a choir or playing a part that is doubled by other instruments would not be suitable for this option.

3. Performing your own composition(s) on the *same* instrument or voice that you presented in Section A. At least one other instrument or voice must be involved – you cannot perform an unaccompanied solo for this option. Again, your programme should be no longer than four minutes and it may consist of just one piece or, at most, two pieces. You must hand a fully-notated

score of your composition(s) to the examiner before you begin your performance.

4. Improvising. The examiner will give you a choice of starting points and you will be allowed ten minutes to prepare. You may use any instrument (or voice). The starting points (some examples of which are shown right) will include:

➢ Four pitches (without rhythm)

➢ A melodic opening (in treble, bass or C-clef) which can be transposed to suit your instrument or voice

➢ A short unpitched rhythm

➢ A chord pattern (for which you may have an accompanist)

➢ A simple poem with an optional melodic opening.

For Section A (and possibly C) you have the option of performing in front of an audience, or in private. The audience cannot stay in the room during the Section B discussion.

Pitch:
Melody:
Rhythm:

Chords:

	F	Dm	Gm	C	
	F^7	Bb	C^7	F	

Poem:

Music, when soft voices die,
Vibrates in the memory –
Odours, when sweet violets sicken,
Live within the sense they thicken.

Rose leaves, when the rose is dead,
Are heaped for the beloved's bed;
And so thy thoughts, when thou art gone,
Love itself shall slumber on.
(Shelley)

Optional opening:

Mu - sic

Preparing for the examination

Perhaps you really enjoy performing in public or perhaps you prefer playing or singing informally with just a small group of friends. You might even be someone who prefers creating your own new music, as a composer. Perhaps you really don't like being in the spotlight and enjoy exploring music by performing it out of earshot of other people. As musicians we all have different interests, strengths and weaknesses: it helps if we are honest with ourselves and recognise what they are, then we can exploit our strengths and work steadily on the bits that don't come quite so naturally. It often turns out to have been worth doing after all.

Even the most experienced international performers have nerves. It is rare for anyone to feel after a concert that it was the 'best I've ever done' – there's nearly always something they think didn't quite come off. Professionals are in a competitive world and always strive to be better – better than they were last year, better than their rivals. If you are hoping to take up a career as a performer then you will have to learn to live with this competitive self-criticism – competing with yourself to improve, competing with others to get the job. Being on top of your technique and knowing the music thoroughly must become a way of life for you.

For many of us, though, exploring music through performing it, interpreting it for ourselves rather than only hearing how other people do it, is one of the most enjoyable parts of developing as a musician. It is a way of getting inside music that will help us understand it better and feed our creative imagination as composers. The more we do, the more we will want to do: if we've got a butterfly nature, impatient to sample everything, we flit from composer to composer, genre to genre; if we tend to stick to one thing then we may get more and more deeply interested in one particular composer or type of music. Most likely you are somewhere in between, always pleased when the opportunity to learn a new piece comes along, but with a good handful of old favourites that you enjoy coming back to. Be curious and adventurous in your study. But, when it comes to an examination, *play safe.*

The performing exam is not a series of hurdles set up to see how far round the course you can get before you fall over: it is designed flexibly, to suit everyone, so that not just different instruments or types of voice are catered for, but different interests in music, different personal temperaments and different circumstances as well. On this occasion *you* choose all the music.

The recital

Choose music you feel comfortable with. Discuss it with your teachers and listen to their advice. If you take lessons with an independent teacher outside your school or college make sure they know what the performing requirements are for OCR AS Music – show them this guide.

Don't rely on a single long piece to give you sufficient scope to show a range of skills and understanding. You need at least one other piece of contrasting music. But *how* contrasting? The music you choose should preferably be typical of the repertoire for the instrument. For instance, if you are a pianist, an arrangement of Pachelbel's *Canon* (originally written for strings and keyboard) is not really typical of piano repertoire and will only give you a very limited opportunity to show your understanding of the instrument. It is usually better to play pieces that were designed with the instrument you are playing in mind.

If you are primarily a jazz performer, 'contrasting' does not mean that you have to perform a Baroque work – you can play entirely jazz pieces, but make sure your programme includes music that uses different techniques and is in different jazz styles.

How difficult? You don't need to torture yourself by playing for a full eight minutes at the most extreme limit of your technical abilities. Include something that shows the best that you can do but remember that 'difficulty' isn't only about pyrotechnics – it's also about expressiveness and understanding the music. Choose at least one piece that lets you show what the instrument can express – perhaps a range of tone colours or dynamics, or a very legato singing line. But don't overreach yourself: what goes well when you are relaxed and totally immersed in the music may throw up unexpected problems when you find yourself in an unfamiliar situation.

It is not a good idea to perform without an accompanist if the music was intended by the composer to be accompanied. As the soloist, you need to be able to show that you can coordinate your solo part with the accompaniment. It is your responsibility to make the arrangements for an accompanist. This should be settled well before the examination date so that you have sufficient time to practise together and become comfortable with one another. You need to hear how the accompaniment goes at an early stage of learning the piece, not in the last few days before the exam. You will feel more secure if you know the accompaniment well – it will help to make your performance much more convincing.

If possible, find out which room or hall the examination will be held in, and try to practise there at least a week in advance. If you are a pianist, you will need plenty of time to get used to the piano in the room. If you play or sing with an accompanist, give your accompanist the opportunity to practise with you using that piano, and sort out where you are going to stand or sit so that you have good eye contact between you. Whether you intend to have an audience on the day or not, try your programme out in front of a group of people – friends, relatives or even the public.

Do all this in good time beforehand so that if unexpected problems arise (you find there's a page-turn that you can't manage without the music falling off the stand, or the noise of the air-conditioning hums distractingly through the quiet bits of the music) something can be done about them.

You will need to have copies of all your music ready to be sent to the examiner at least a week before the recital. Photocopies may be used. They will be taken away by the examiner for reference.

> The examiner's copies of your music will be returned later (or destroyed, in the case of photocopies).

Discussion

The examiner will be interested to find out what you thought about as you prepared each piece – how you made your expressive choices, why you decided to perform a particular passage one way rather than another and whether you think it worked as intended in the performance you've just given. It is not about how many notes you slipped up on, or which bits were too difficult for you – you are not being asked to confess to performing badly – but about aspects of the music that may be less obvious: if you got faster somewhere in the middle of a piece, was this because the composer had marked it accelerando or because you felt the music really needed to push on at that particular moment? If the dynamic markings range from pp to ff, do you think the contrasts were sufficiently effective? What made you put that particular ornament in this phrase? Why did you slur the last two bars that way?

We practise writing about music, learn technical terms, and develop new skills to identify and describe what we hear. But talking about our own performance is not something we are often encouraged to do. In our lessons the usual routine is probably: you play, your teacher listens and then does the talking. And, much of the time, because we respect our teacher's judgement, if they say 'no, play the phrase this way' and then they demonstrate for you to copy, we do it: have you ever asked 'why'? 'Why?' is what the examiner is going to want to discover from you.

How can you practise for this part of the examination? Start by listening more closely to your friends when they perform and by trying to articulate a more detailed response than you would usually – not just 'that was great', but 'I liked the beginning and the end very much but am not so sure about the middle'. This might lead to a discussion about the effect that their performance had and you could both try to tease out why the outside parts were exciting but that middle bit was boring or dull or just lost momentum. Then invite them for a return match to listen to you and discuss your performance. This isn't enough for the discussion in the exam, but it's a way to get started thinking about why performances are the way they are – not just because your teachers have said 'do it my way' – and how people sometimes hear what we perform quite differently from what we assumed.

In Section B of the listening paper you will be asked to compare two different performances of a passage from one of the set orchestral scores or be asked questions about the performing style and technique of one of the musicians in the set jazz recordings. Reflecting on your own performing intentions and how effectively they came over in performance is the other side of this coin: when performing, *you* are the interpreter.

Extended performing

The decision about which of the four options you are going to do needs to be taken fairly early. There are a number of practical considerations. Discuss all of the options thoroughly with your teachers before deciding.

If you are thinking of doing option 1 (performing on a second instrument or voice) the choice about which instrument to offer for the Section A recital and which one to offer here can be a tricky one if you are equally strong on both of them. Bear in mind that there are only 40 marks for this part of the examination, while the Section A recital is worth 60 marks. It makes sense to offer your stronger instrument in Section A.

If you want to take option 2 (performing in an ensemble or duet, or as an accompanist), then other performers will be involved and you need to begin to make arrangements for rehearsals as early as possible. Choosing and obtaining suitable music (particularly if your ensemble is not a common combination of instruments) may take longer than you expect. It needs to be something that everyone involved can manage comfortably, but that also stretches you (remember that your part must not be doubled by anyone else).

You also need to give yourself plenty of time to try out your different role – for example, you may never have accompanied anyone before and your soloist's choice of music might challenge you more than you expected. This option puts you into a different relationship with other performers – this time you are not the 'star performer' and you may have to learn some negotiating skills. Be prepared for some setbacks: if you are working with other students, they will be under pressure too, and your examination may not be at the top of their agenda. Agree a manageable rehearsal schedule in good time and stick to it.

If you choose option 3 (performing your own composition), you will obviously need to start drafting ideas, and then refining and completing the actual composition well before the examination.

You may use any instrument, or singing, for option 4 (improvising): it doesn't have to be the instrument you used in your recital. You may have no difficulty deciding which of the starting points is likely to be best for you. If you are a singer, it is sensible to choose the poem; if you're a guitarist, the chords; a drummer, the rhythm.

If you play a melody or keyboard instrument, you have more choice. A saxophone player, for instance, might choose the pitches, the melodic opening, the rhythm, or even the chords. If you play a melody instrument such as the flute and choose the chords as a starting point, you can have an accompanist to play the chords. The accompanist is allowed to practise with you in the ten-minute preparation time but is not allowed to help you with your own improvisation. If you are a keyboard player and choose the chords option, you are not allowed to play with another performer.

On the day

You will be told the date of the examination in advance. The examiner will contact your teacher, probably during February, to arrange a time that is convenient for everyone. It may be before the end of the spring term or early in the summer term. Your teacher will draw up a timetable for the day and ask you for details of your programme. It is your responsibility to make sure that your accompanist, if you need one, and any other performers needed for your Section C option, all know the date and time, and confirm that they will be available.

The day before the examination, make sure that everything is organised – copies of the music, music stands, amplifiers and an audience, if you want one. Practise carefully in a quiet frame of mind, and have a good sleep. On the day, keep calm – let yourself breathe. Think positively – the examiner is not the enemy or an alien species. He or she is a musician, probably a teacher and possibly a parent as well, who understands the stress you are under. Very occasionally it may be a surprise when you walk into the examination room to find that that there are two examiners. This is done to make sure that examiners are all marking to the same standard across the country. It doesn't put you under twice as much as pressure!

The whole examination will be recorded – this is a safeguard for you.

The examiner will probably say something welcoming when you come into the room. Listen carefully to everything the examiner says but don't try to read too much into it. If you are asked to wait a few moments between pieces, don't assume that what you've just done was so terrible that a whole essay is being written about it. If you've chosen a programme that goes on too long and the examiner stops you, don't jump to the conclusion that he or she couldn't stand any more – they are probably being very careful to keep to the timetable so that the next student is not kept waiting.

However carefully you've prepared, though, the unexpected can always happen – the fire alarm goes, a string breaks, your accompanist is ill and someone else stands in at the last moment. None of these signals the end of the world. Examiners have these things happen to them in their own day-to-day work as musicians and they understand the extra stress it puts you under. Don't panic – deal with the problem and carry on.

Assessment

Most of us are naturally self-critical about our performing. The desire to improve is healthy and makes us practise but, because we're trying to get it 'right', we sometimes get into a habit of paying more attention to what is 'wrong' than what is going well. The job of our teachers, especially, is to point out what needs attention and how to overcome problems: we may sometimes feel that we can never satisfy them. This can result in our reflections about how we performed focusing too much on the negative aspects, always remembering what went wrong, instead of what worked well.

The job of an examiner is different from that of a teacher. It is to notice everything that you *can* do. Right from the start the examiner will be listening in a positive way, giving marks for what you achieve, not taking them away because of things that didn't go well. Examiners work to marking criteria that specify the range of marks available for various levels of performance. As you will see below, it is not just getting all the notes right that matters, there are other aspects of your performance that the examiner will consider.

The full marking criteria for Performing, along with detailed descriptions of the mark bands, are printed in Appendix B of the OCR Specification.

Recital

Each of the following four categories of assessment is worth 15 of the total 60 marks available for the recital.

Knowledge and fluency (of pitch and rhythm)

This is an assessment of how well you know the music, how securely you have it in your head. Although it's partly about getting all the notes right, it's more about whether you are confident about where the music is going. If your fingers slip through nerves and the examiner feels that you nevertheless knew what you should have played, the 'fluff' will probably be overlooked.

This also applies if part of your performance involves improvisation: in this case it's not so much about accuracy as whether your musical ideas are fluent and what you play has a sense of direction.

Technical control

You may have learned the music thoroughly and understand a lot about how it ought to go, but can you actually get through it without falling over in passages that are really too difficult for you? This would be an obvious sign that you are not in technical control of your instrument (in this respect the voice is an 'instrument', too).

Although you want to show the very best of what you can do, it is always a mistake to perform music that you are not quite on top of. It will make you extra edgy when you really want to be able to concentrate on all the other aspects that matter. But the examiner will be listening for more than just whether you can perform the correct notes: a wide range of technical skills can be rewarded, some of them quite subtle, like balance between melody and chords or contrasts of tone-colours, as well as more obvious aspects like intonation, pedalling, breathing, tonguing or diction. Try to choose music that allows you to show different technical and expressive skills. If you are a pianist, include something that shows you can use the sustaining pedal, but don't play a whole programme of over-pedalled pieces; if you're a singer, make sure that you show you can sustain a melodic line without help from the piano – don't choose a programme that consists entirely of songs in which the accompaniment doubles the vocal part.

For most of us, the first category of marks, Knowledge and fluency, will be about knowing what the composer wrote on the page – the notes and rhythms. The marks under the third category, Realisation of performance markings and/or performing conventions, are for showing in your performing that you understand other sorts of signs such as tempo and dynamic markings, articulation, ornaments and some of the aspects of music that are not written down – the conventions associated with different types of music. These might include, for instance, playing quavers in a swung style in jazz, or deliberately unevenly (*notes inégales*) in some types of Baroque music, or adopting a flexible approach to tempo (*rubato*) where appropriate in Romantic music. In other words, the examiner will be listening to hear whether you are performing the music in the way that the composer would have expected it to sound.

Realisation of performance markings and/or performing conventions

Do you actually listen to the sounds you are making or are you too busy worrying about what comes next? If your intonation is a bit off, is it because you're not really listening to yourself or because, technically, you can't play it any more accurately? If you came in too soon, was it due to not knowing the music well enough or was it because you weren't listening to the accompaniment? And do you understand the different styles needed for a Bach minuet and a Chopin waltz, or a Mozart aria and a Lloyd Webber song? This is where your *musicianship* really shows.

Aural and stylistic understanding

Discussion

The better you understand the styles of your pieces and know what to consider when performing them, then the more detailed you can be in your answers and so more of the 20 available marks can be awarded. If you want to, you can illustrate particular points by playing or singing a phrase or passage that you are discussing, *provided that it is relevant*. For instance, you might want to show that you had thought about which notes in a phrase to slur and which ones to detach: it could be appropriate to demonstrate and then discuss the differences, in order to explain why you chose to perform it the way you did.

Key phrases in OCR's description of the sort of discussion that would be worth between 13 and 16 of the 20 marks are: 'informed answers', 'clear awareness of expressive choices ... and of their effectiveness in performance'.

Although you will have no idea beforehand what questions about your performance the examiner will ask, you can be sure that there will be no trick questions designed to catch you out. The examiner will be keen to find what you *can* talk about – your communication skills are not being assessed and you will not lose marks just because you stumble over a word. And you have every reason to feel confident because *you* have chosen the music. You are not going to be asked about unfamiliar music. Provided you have thought about what you are doing, and why, as you prepared, and haven't been performing parrot-fashion or on autopilot, you should feel that you are on home territory.

Extended performing

The marking criteria for the various extended performing options are mostly similar to those for the recital.

Second instrument or voice

The criteria for this option are identical to those for the recital, except that each of the four categories is marked out of ten rather than 15 marks.

Duet, ensemble or accompanying

This option requires extra aural and stylistic awareness – listening to the other performer(s), coordinating, knowing when to come to the fore and when to blend. In an improvisatory style (like a jazz group) the ability to extend musical ideas in a way that is appropriate to the style also comes into the picture. If a group uses amplifiers, the way they are managed to balance the performance may also be taken into account.

Your own composition(s)

This option is assessed in a similar way to Section B of the composing unit. There are ten marks for the score and the accuracy of its relationship to what is performed; ten marks for the way the composition shows your understanding of the technical and expressive possibilities of your instrument (or voice); a further ten marks for similar understanding of the other instruments or voices involved in the composition; and ten marks for the way the composition shows your aural awareness and understanding of the relationship between all the performers in the ensemble.

Notice that many of the marks in this option are awarded for composing skills. If composition is your strength, this is the place in the course where you could capitalise on it.

Improvising

For your improvisation there are ten marks available for fluency and form, ten for technical control, ten for imaginative use of the 'stimulus' (the starting point), and ten for your aural and stylistic awareness.

The areas of study

Two areas of study have important roles in underpinning large sections of your AS course – ideas, techniques and various bits of information that relate to them will keep cropping up. You will find it helpful to keep them in mind in almost everything you do. Get your ears tuned in to recognising their relevance in whatever you are performing, composing or listening to.

Tonality (The Language of Western Tonal Harmony)

Don't confuse tonality with 'tone colour', which means something completely different. Music that is **tonal** is music that uses one or more keys (as in major or minor).

The word **tonic** refers to the main key of a piece of music and its key chord (chord I). A piece of tonal music usually begins and ends in its tonic key and will probably pass through other keys (**modulate**) in between. These other keys are described as **related** if they contain many notes in common with the tonic – for example, the relative minor shares the same key signature as its relative major key – otherwise they are said to be **non-related**. Relationships between keys play an important structural role in a great deal of the music that you will hear and perform.

If the pitches in tonal music all come from the current key, the music is said to be **diatonic**. Pitches outside the current key that are used to add colour rather than to introduce a modulation, are called **chromatic** notes (chromatic means 'coloured').

The major and minor scales of the tonal system are not the only scales used in music. For example, until about 1600 various **modes** were used in European music. Some folk songs are modal, and a number of 19th- and 20th-century composers have used modes in their music to give it a folk or national flavour. Major and minor scales are sometimes thought of as two modes that survived after 1600.

By the end of the 19th century, tonal harmony had become so complex that a clear sense of related keys became increasingly obscured by the use of many chromatic notes. In the 20th century some composers experimented with non-tonal types of scale as a basis for organising their compositions. Today, some music is tonal and some is non-tonal. In your own work for Section B of the composing unit (and for the composing option in Section C of the performing unit) you are free to choose tonal or non-tonal styles, but your exercises for Composing Section A must be tonal.

The rejection of tonality by some composers after 1900 is sometimes described as the 'breakdown of tonality'. Of course, it did not actually die out. Many composers have continued to write in a broadly tonal style, and much western popular music (and even jazz) is essentially tonal in nature.

The word 'western' reminds us that it is mainly in the history of European (and later, American) music that tonality has had such a dominant role. Other civilisations (such as India and Japan) have used different systems. In Indian music, a *raga* sets out the melodic ingredients from which an improvisation will grow. As it progresses the audience recognises and appreciates the performer's uniquely personal expressive use of characteristic features of the *raga*.

In a similar way, although most of us are unaware of it as we listen to western tonal repertoire, we orientate ourselves at the beginning of a piece by fixing the tonic in our ears as 'the place we are starting from', and then recognise and enjoy the way the music travels away from it and comes home again at the end – a satisfying resolution to the story.

In a loose way we often use the metaphor of a language to describe the way tonality works. The parts of this language that you need to learn to handle confidently – the chords, cadences, modulations, passing notes and so on – are a little bit like parts of speech (nouns, verbs, conjunctions). This may be a useful way to think about the techniques and conventions but it doesn't mean that 16 bars of music will have a meaning in the way that a sentence does.

The specific features of western tonal harmony that you must learn to recognise and be able to handle are:

➢ Major and minor keys

➢ Diatonic intervals (major or minor 3rds and 6ths etc)

➢ Chords I to VII and their inversions; chords with an added 7th

➢ Perfect, imperfect, plagal and interrupted cadences, and other common chord progressions

➢ Modulation to closely-related keys (dominant, subdominant and the relative minor or relative major)

➢ Tonal devices such as sequence and pedal.

Above all you need to learn to recognise the harmonic implications of a melody or bass, and to develop a feel for how often the harmonies change (known as the **rate of harmonic change** or **harmonic rhythm**).

All the work you do in Section A of the composing unit is based on this area of study, and it also plays a large part in Sections A and B of the listening paper. Much of the music that you perform will also be in tonal styles, whether from the 17th, 18th, 19th or 20th centuries: understanding its tonal language will help you find suitable ways to shape such pieces expressively.

As we study the music of the 18th century we will become aware of various conventions – things that were common practice, although never 'rules'. For example, it was common for a piece to begin by making the tonic clear to the listener, perhaps by basing the melody on parts of a broken chord. But it was inevitable that one day somebody would have the idea of starting in a different, more ambiguous way.

In the exam, chord names may be given as well as Roman numerals (e.g. VI/Gm).

The Expressive Use of Instrumental Techniques

If you took GCSE Music you will have learned something about individual instruments and the sounds that they are able to make, and you will already know quite a lot about the one you play yourself. In this area of study you learn more about performing techniques and how musicians use them for expressive effects. You will also learn about ways of *combining* instruments to produce different textures and sonorities.

Although this area of study is about instruments, if you are a singer it's worth thinking about vocal techniques in a similar way.

As a starting point, see what more you can discover about your own instrument: it may be able to do a great deal more than you are capable of producing on it at the moment. Listen to well-known performers. When you are sure you know your instrument inside out, compare it with similar instruments in terms of its range, registers (the different parts of the range), timbres (tone colours), agility and expressive power.

Your study of three orchestral scores and three jazz recordings for the listening paper will focus a great deal on techniques of performing and on ways of combining instruments. When you come to compose your own music for instrumental ensemble in Section B of the composing unit, the sounds you have been listening to, and the understanding you have gained about how these are produced, will provide you with a stock of techniques that you can draw on. You won't want to compose an 18th-century symphony or a 1920s' jazz standard – your own musical language will be different – but the textures and timbres you have studied may well be ones that linger in your imagination.

These pieces also provide the focus for your historical study: many instruments in the 18th century looked and sounded very different from the way they do now. You need to know about this. But there is also a great difference in the way composers scored for them at the beginning of the 18th century (Vivaldi) and a hundred years later (Beethoven). Even during Haydn's lifetime the instruments themselves were changing. Jazz hasn't stood still, either: you will discover differences between the sounds that performers made in the 1920s and only 30 years later, even on the same type of instrument.

In your own performing, too, particularly if you are playing in an ensemble or singing in a choir, get into the habit of noticing who is doing what – playing or singing in unison, 3rds, imitation, contributing to widely- or tightly-spaced chords, throwing a motif from part to part in dialogue, presenting the melody in the lowest part and so on. Notice details of articulation, dynamics, phrasing and balance.

Composing

The skills of composing can be learned in a similar way to performing: building technical knowledge and understanding; exploring good role models; regular practice – all with the final aim of presenting your ideas in a musically satisfying way.

The craft of composing involves making choices:

➢ Selecting (considering) the raw materials of sound

➢ Choosing sound sources and timbres

➢ Shaping theses sources into 'building blocks'

➢ Modifying, extending, transforming, organising and assembling to create a piece of music.

Harmony is one of the key elements of music composition. The triad is central to western tonal harmony. You may already have learned something about chords and keys, either from GCSE Music or in studying for a music theory exam. It is also possible to learn a great deal about tonal harmony by being inquisitive and curious about the music you play and listen to. The music itself becomes your textbook.

The two sections in this coursework unit carry equal marks. Your final portfolio will contain:

➢ **Section A: The Language of Western Tonal Harmony** (45 marks)

A minimum of seven exercises, including one completed under timed conditions.

➢ **Section B: Instrumental Techniques** (45 marks)

A composition or arrangement for between four and ten instruments with a maximum length of three minutes.

At first glance, the two sections of this unit may appear to be quite separate in their demands. The work in Section A will enable you to become familiar with the practices and conventions of tonality (a system that has been the backbone of western music for several centuries). Section B allows for a more personal extension of your composing ideas. Many of the basic concepts studied in Section A will be relevant to your work for Section B, whatever choices of language, style or genre you make. Both involve studying music by established composers to use as models of best composing practice.

> Your teacher, who is responsible for monitoring your work throughout the course, will mark your composition portfolio. Samples of work from your centre will be sent to OCR to ensure that the assessment is fair and meets the required standards.

Section A: Western Tonal Harmony

> The melodies in the exercises you actually submit must either be by named composers or be traditional melodies or folksongs – they cannot be tunes specially written for practice purposes.

To begin with, your teacher may introduce you to the basics through shorter exercises. These exercises may include 'sign-posts' to help you with harmonic or textural decisions. As you become more confident you should be able to work independently without hints or prompts.

Your exercises will consist of a complete melody plus the opening notes of the complete texture. This is sometimes referred to as the 'incipit'. The melodies used must be by established composers. You will consider the harmonies suggested by the music, derive a suitable bass part and write in chord symbols to show your understanding of the choices you make. In at least two exercises you will need to show the harmonies in full with a complete texture based on the model of the given opening.

It is essential to hear the music you are working with in this unit. The exercises in this study guide will help ensure that the concepts described come to life in a practical way for you. Your teacher will often play examples to you. You may also want to consult any of the harmony textbooks listed for extra preliminary exercises and further help.

An explanation of the timed exercise, along with advice on the selection of your final six exercises, are given on pages 40–41.

AS Music Harmony Workbook by Hugh Benham. Rhinegold, 2008, ISBN 978-1-906178-34-5.

Harmony in Practice by Anna Butterworth. ABRSM Publishing, 1999, ISBN 978-1-854728-33-3.

The ABC of Harmony series by Roy Wilkinson. Boosey and Hawkes.

The Dynamics of Harmony: Principles and Practice by George Pratt. Oxford University Press, 1984/1996, ISBN 978-0-198790-20-4.

Harmony by Walter Piston. W. W. Norton & Co. Ltd, 1988, ISBN 978-0-393-95480-7.

Getting started

You will need a working understanding of staff notation in both treble and bass clefs. If your reading skills are not very fluent do not worry: with practice you will improve and the rewards are well worth the effort. In addition you will need to know about:

➢ Keys, intervals, scales

➢ Chords and cadences.

Remember that working with chords, bass lines and melodies is a musical activity: try not to view it as 'theory'. Take every opportunity to observe what is happening in the music by using your ears and eyes as well as developing your understanding.

In questions for your historical unit, you will need to identify keys, modulations and individual chords, and be able to analyse sections of the harmonic structure.

Understanding chords

A method of labelling the degrees of the scale on which the triads are formed was developed in the early 19th century; this method uses Roman numerals beneath the stave. This chapter will use: upper case numerals for major chords; lower case for minor; italics for other types of chord.

A checklist is provided on page 42 to help you make sure that your portfolio includes a suitable range of skills and understanding.

Each triad is made up of 3rds superimposed on each degree of the scale. These are described as 'root position' chords.

You will notice that two of the chords, ii and V, have a further third superimposed above the triad: counting from the root note, it is a 7th above. Chords with an added 7th are a common feature of the harmonic language of western music.

Chord voicing

The triads in the previous example are in **close position**; their notes are as close together as possible. Play them through slowly on a keyboard instrument; first without the added 7th on ii and V, and then with it included. Can you hear that some of the triads sound major and some minor? The triad on the leading note is a diminished triad and sounds rather different.

The harmony will sound more effective if the notes of the chord are more widely spaced in what is called open position. The way the notes are distributed in a chord is called the voicing. There are many possibilities when using open position chords; some different voicings of a C major chord are shown left.

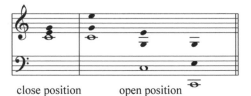

close position   open position

So long as the degree of the scale on which the triad is built remains at the bottom of the chord, the chord is said to be in root position – no matter how many notes there are above or how they are arranged. When a different note of the chord is in the bass, the chord is known as an inverted chord. If the:

➤ 3rd of the chord is in the bass (the lowest note), the chord is in **first inversion**

➤ 5th of the chord is in the bass (the lowest note), the chord is in **second inversion**

➤ 7th of the chord is in the bass (the lowest note), the chord is in **third inversion.**

Notice in the following example (in D major) how each chord inversion is indicated by adding 'b', 'c' or 'd' to the Roman numeral that describes the chord:

D major: I   Ib   Ic   IV   IVb   IVc   V   Vb   Vc   V⁷d

Chords in root position, and in first or third inversion, are freely used when harmonising melodies; second inversions are used less freely and in the special circumstances described on page 34.

If you are a guitarist or jazz pianist you may be familiar with a different style of chord labelling, positioned above the stave. This system of notation uses the letter name of the root of the chord. If a letter name appears by itself it is assumed to be major. If the triad is minor, the letter name is followed by 'm' or 'min', while 'dim' after the letter indicates a diminished triad. Inversions are shown by writing the chord name followed by an oblique symbol – or forward slash '/' – and then the name of the bass note. For example, C/E is a first inversion chord of C major, with E as the lowest note in the bass. In some of the examples that follow both systems are used.

Why are there two methods for labelling chords? Roman numerals show the function of the chord in relationship to the given key: for example, a chord V is always the dominant chord whatever key the music is in at that point. Letter names show immediately what notes are to be played regardless of the overall key: if the chord is C, you play C, E, and G.

Exercise 1

1. On a keyboard instrument – right hand only – play some triads in their various root and inverted positions in as many keys as you can. Play through the example below to begin with, and then move to some other keys.

2. Play and label each of the triads in the examples below. Use either Roman numerals or chord symbols, and show the type of inversion when the chord is not in root position. The first answer is given.

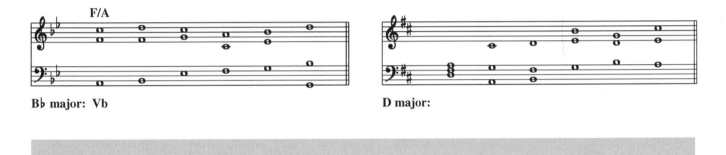

Bb major: Vb   D major:

Harmonising melodies

There is a great deal of flexibility in the choice and type of melodies that can be worked for the Section A exercises. This allows you to start from your own experience and performing abilities. You should also aim to cover new ground as you explore the range of music that uses western tonal harmony. Some examples of suitable material might include:

➤ Traditional folk songs

➤ Simple popular songs from the 19th and early 20th centuries

➤ 18th-century keyboard pieces

➤ Hymn settings

➤ Early classical string quartets

➤ Short, simple pieces from the Romantic period.

You may begin by working with well-known melodies. For later exercises, however, it is best to avoid tunes that you are aurally very familiar with because these do not allow you to make judgements about the choice of harmony for yourself.

Melodies in a major key   The melody of a piece contains many clues about the harmony and bass line possibilities. When harmonising a melody for the first time, familiarity with the melody is a very important starting point: play or sing it through several times.

Amazing Grace

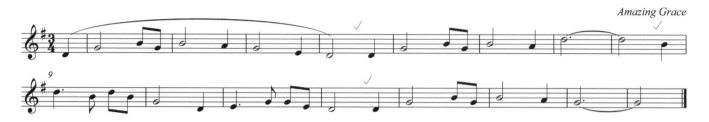

Using the example above, aim to get a sense of the phrase lengths and where the cadence points lie at the end of each phrase. A phrase is often likened to a sentence. As in this example, it is useful to mark the ends of phrases with a tick (the place where a singer would take a breath) and / or draw a phrase mark in the appropriate place on the score.

Exercise 2

1. Copy out the notes of the melody for *Amazing Grace*, from the example above.

2. Notice how each of the four phrases begins with an **anacrusis** (upbeat) of one crotchet beat before the bar line. Draw in the phrase marks and indicate the end of each phrase with a tick.

3. Your ear will often guide you as you think about where the harmony should change. Sing or play the melody with an accompaniment of a single tonic chord of G throughout (strummed guitar or piano vamp); it should feel 'uncomfortable' at those places in the melody where the harmony needs to be changed.

Selecting chords in a major key   The melody for *Amazing Grace* is in the key of G major. The example below shows the range of (diatonic) chords available in G major to harmonise this melody.

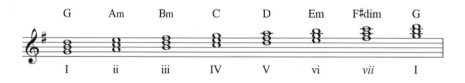

At this point, your first question is: 'Which chords should I use?' In both major and minor keys, chords I, IV and V are known as the **primary triads**, as they are the most commonly used chords in harmony. The most important triad of all is I, the tonic chord, which shares the letter name of the key. Many pieces start and finish on the tonic chord. The second most important chord is V, the dominant chord. The most commonly used **secondary triads** are ii and vi, although chord iii is also occasionally used. In a major key, chords I, IV and V are **major** triads, and chords ii, iii and vi are **minor** triads.

The earlier section on 'Understanding chords' in this chapter (page 21) introduced briefly the concept of **7th chords**. Adding the 7th above the root of a triad results in a four-note chord. The two most common 7th chords are those on the dominant (V⁷) and the supertonic (ii⁷). The **dominant 7th** is often used instead of a plain dominant triad in a perfect cadence, V⁷–I; it is one of the strongest ways to confirm the tonality of a piece of music. Chord ii⁷ often precedes V⁷ at a cadential point: ii⁷–V⁽⁷⁾–I.

Understanding the function of primary and secondary triads within a key opens up a basic framework to harmonise a melody. Therefore, you now have the following chords to draw from for your harmonisation of *Amazing Grace* in the key of G major:

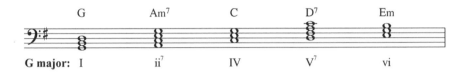

We have already noted that cadences 'punctuate' the phrases of a melody, just as punctuation separates clauses and sentences in English grammar. The two most commonly used are:

Cadences

➢ The **perfect cadence** consists of the progression V–I at the end of a phrase and brings a temporary or permanent halt to the music (like a 'full stop')

➢ The **imperfect cadence** uses any chord (I, ii, iib, and IV are the most frequent possibilities) followed by chord V at the end of a phrase. This cadence has an inconclusive effect rather like a comma; the music has more to say.

Two other cadences occuring less frequently are:

➢ The **plagal cadence** has a conclusive effect and consists of the chords IV–I. It is sometimes likened to the sound of a sung 'Amen' in sacred choral music

➢ The **interrupted cadence** is most usually represented by the progression V–vi. The harmonic flow (or pull) towards the tonic has been interrupted. This cadence is often used to build tension in a piece of music, in anticipation of a proceeding, stronger perfect cadence to confirm the tonic key.

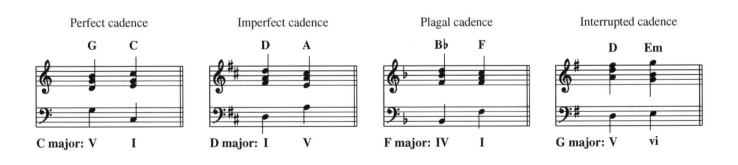

Exercise 3

Listen to and follow with your score the fourth movement of Haydn's Symphony No. 103. Identify as many examples of a perfect cadence as you can. Identify instances that confirm the tonality of the movement (E♭ major) and those that indicate a change of key (modulation).

Melodies in a minor key

Below is an example of a traditional English melody in a minor key. Included in this example is an 'incipit' – a starting point that provides plucked guitar chords for you to continue in a similar style. To harmonise this melody, approach it in the same way as covered in the preceding section on major keys. Namely, sing or play the melody to become familiar with it; identify the key; mark in the phrases and the cadence points; and then identify the diatonic primary and secondary triads that could be used to harmonise the melody. (As you become familiar with the melody, you may recognise with your ears that there is a key change after the repeat of the first phrase at bar 5.)

Traditional English: *The Miller of Dee*

Relative keys

At first glance you might think that *The Miller of Dee*, with a key signature of a single flat, is in the key of F major. However, remember that every key signature has two possibilities: a major key and a relative minor key. The tonic of the relative minor is three semitones lower than the tonic of the major key. The D in bars 1 and 12, together with the raised 7th (C♯), confirm that *The Miller of Dee* is in D minor rather than F major.

Minor scales

There are two main types of minor scale: **harmonic minor** and **melodic minor**. The following three examples use a key signature of a single flat to illustrate the relationship between the relative keys.

D melodic minor

As the name suggests, the harmonic minor scale is the one used primarily for writing harmony in the minor key. Notice that the 7th degree (leading note) is raised by a semitone, and that the ascending and descending versions of the melodic minor scale are slightly different. On the way up, both the 6th and the 7th degrees are raised by a semitone. However, on the way down both notes are restored to their 'natural' pitches (in other words, using only the pitches of the relative major key). As its name suggests, the melodic minor is preferred for melody writing because it avoids the awkward sound of the interval of the augmented 2nd between the 6th and 7th notes of the harmonic minor scale. (In D harmonic minor, the augmented 2nd is B♭ to C♯.)

Exercise 4

In the first movement of Vivaldi's E minor Bassoon Concerto, minor scales patterns are a very important aspect of the compositional texture. When analysing the score, notice how Vivaldi always uses the minor 3rd of the scale but presents us with every possible combination of 'harmonic' and 'melodic' 6th and 7th degrees of the scale.

1. Write out the scales found in:

    ➢ bar 2, second violin

    ➢ bars 5–6, first and second violin

    ➢ bars 23–24, solo bassoon.

    In bar 26, notice how the second violin part has a descending version of the ascending melodic minor scale.

2. Choose a minor scale that you can play on your instrument. Play the related major scale and then the two versions of the minor scale (one octave for each scale, ascending and descending) until you are really familiar with the difference in sound between them. Play these three related scales in different rhythms: for example, try using a dotted rhythm or the reverse 'snap' ('Lombardic' rhythm) that Vivaldi uses in his concerto (for example bar 2, violin 2).

> One edition of Vivaldi's Bassoon Concerto in E minor counts the anacrusis (upbeat) as bar 1 and the first full bar as bar 2. For the purposes of this study guide the anacrusis bar is regarded as bar 0⁴ and the first full bar as bar 1.

The function of chords is to support and complement the melody. Therefore, each minor chord has to be adaptable so that it can fit with melody notes from either the melodic or the harmonic minor scale. The stave below shows some of the most frequent versions of chords that can be used in the minor keys, using D minor as an example. (Chord VI, a major chord in a minor key, can often be used with stunning effect.)

Selecting chords in a minor key

> Your portfolio should include at least one exercise in a minor key. The melody should be clearly minor – avoid folk tunes such as *Scarborough Fair* and *Greensleeves* that are modal rather than minor.

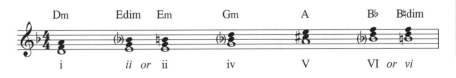

If you need to use a diminished triad, a good tip is to remember that it works best in first inversion with a doubled 3rd – the same applies to chord vii in major and minor keys.

Harmonic rhythm

The rate at which the harmony changes in relation to the melody is called the **harmonic rhythm**. In hymns and chorales (German hymn tunes) chords usually change on almost every beat of the bar. But in other types of melody the harmony usually changes less frequently – perhaps two chords a bar (for example, the opening of Vivaldi's bassoon concerto), perhaps only one, and in some cases the same chord may extend over two or more bars.

Up to half of the exercises in your portfolio can be harmonisations of hymn or chorale melodies, if you wish. But the remainder should show different rates of harmonic rhythm where you have to think carefully about the best places to make chord changes.

Sometimes the rate of harmonic change will increase at important cadences. If you look at the Welsh melody below, *The Ash Grove*, you will notice that only one chord per bar is needed for most of the tune (and a tonic chord could be used for the whole of bars 1–2). However, two different chords are needed in bar 7 to prepare for the perfect cadence in the final two bars.

Welsh Air: *The Ash Grove*

Exercise 5

1. Harmonise the following melody by writing a suitable chord in each box, either above or below the stave using the appropriate symbols. Think carefully about which chord would work best before the perfect cadence at the end of the phrase.

Amazing Grace

2. Choose suitable chords for the following melody by writing appropriate symbols in the correct positions either above or below the stave. The first two bars have been completed for you – notice that each chord lasts for two crotchet beats, and that a chord is placed on the rest at the start of bar 2. There is no need to increase the harmonic rhythm at the final cadence for this melody.

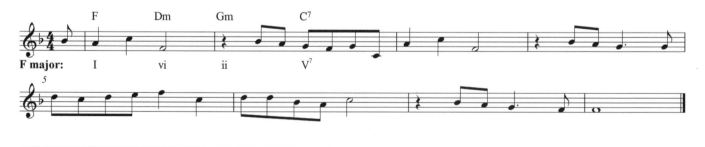

Melodies can contain harmonic 'clues' by including broken-chord patterns as part of their structure.

Non-harmony melody notes

J. S. Bach: Minuet in G

This example is in G major, the primary triads of which are shown right for reference. The melody implies harmony very clearly. The first four notes in bar 1 belong to chord I, while the next two could be harmonised with chord V (requiring D in the bass). The tonic is emphasised in bar 2, so a return to chord I would be better here than using chord IV (which also contains the tonic). Bars 3–4 are a repeat of the first two bars. In bar 5 there are only two notes, E and G. If we add C as a bass note, we have all the notes of chord IV. Which chord is suggested by bar 6?

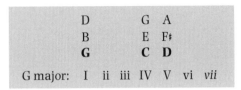

Melodies based entirely on harmony notes can result in rather angular contours caused by the many **leaps** involved. Most tunes create a smoother outline by including **stepwise movement**:

Petzold / J. S. Bach: Minuet in G

The five notes in bar 1 are not contained in any one chord, so it is necessary to deduce which notes are harmony notes and which are not. We know that many tonal pieces begin with the tonic chord, which in G major has the notes G–B–D. In bar 1 of the Minuet example, the notes D, G and B fall on the first, second and third beats of the bar, respectively. Therefore, chord I is the obvious choice for bar 1.

The notes printed in grey (in bars 1 and 3) are not part of the chord for that bar; they are known as 'non-harmony notes'.

The non-harmony notes in the Minuet example are known as **passing notes** because they pass by stepwise movement between the notes of the chord. Passing notes always move by step. They never leap to or from harmony notes, and they usually occur in rhythmically weak positions (here on quavers, after beats 2 and 3). As a result the passing dissonances they create are hardly noticeable.

> You may find that 'non-harmony notes' are referred to elsewhere as 'inessential notes' or 'embellishing notes'.

Sometimes passing notes fall on the beat, in which case they are described as **accented passing notes**. Such notes also move by step between harmony notes. However, because accented passing notes occur on the beat, the dissonance they produce against the underlying chord is more noticeable and often very expressive. The example in the right margin shows the accented passing notes circled. When the dissonant note moves by step to a harmony note we say it has **resolved**.

Mozart: Rondo, K. 485

G major: I

Auxiliaries:

Auxiliary notes decorate or embellish the harmony notes by moving to the note above (an upper auxiliary) or below (a lower auxiliary) and then back again.

In the example given in the left margin, the auxiliary notes fall rhythmically on the weak parts of the beat. If the non-harmony notes have accidentals, we refer to them as **chromatic auxiliary notes**. In the example that follows, from Beethoven's Violin Concerto in D major (first movement, bars 396–398), the chromatic auxiliary notes fall on the stronger points of each beat.

Draw circles around the harmony notes in the solo violin part so that you can clearly identify the chromatic auxiliary notes.

Appoggiatura:

Another type of non-harmony note is the **appoggiatura**. The appoggiatura is similar to the accented passing note, except that it is approached by a leap rather than by step.

The extract below illustrates an appoggiatura, taken from the first movement of Vivaldi's Bassoon Concerto in E minor, bar 17.

In this example, the bassoon melody leaps down to a G in beat 3; this note is not a harmony note of the D major chord in the editor's keyboard continuo part. It creates an expressive, dissonant effect that is then resolved as the melody drops down to the harmony note, F♯ on the weaker final crotchet beat of the bar.

Suspension:

A similar non-harmony note, which creates a delay in the sounding of all the pitches of a chord together, is the **suspension**. A suspension occurs when a harmony note from a previous chord is held on or repeated while a new chord is sounded beneath it (rather than jumping to the dissonance, as in the appoggiatura). The prolonged note is described as a 'preparation'. When the chord beneath it changes, the held note becomes the 'suspension', which creates a dissonance with the new underlying harmony. The dissonant note then moves by step to a note of the new chord, which creates a 'resolution'.

> To help remember the difference between an appoggiatura and a suspension, remember that a suspension must always include 'preparation, suspension, resolution'; whereas an appoggiatura has no preparation note and does not have to be approached by step.

Exercise 6

The first phrase of the traditional melody below has a flowing accompaniment pattern.

1. Within the melody, identify the: harmony notes; passing notes; and a preparation note for a suspension that follows.

Traditional: *Flow Gently Sweet Afton*

2. Add in the correct chord symbols beneath the bass stave.

3. Using your ear (and/or an instrument to help), notate a simple melody and harmonise it with appropriate chord symbols: for example, the first eight bars of *Skip to My Lou*. Once you have it sketched out, decorate the melody by including the following embellishments: passing notes, upper/lower (chromatic) auxiliaries and suspensions.

Writing a bass part

With your key, melody and chords decided, the next element to consider when harmonising a melody is writing a bass part. A simple bass line can be derived from the root notes of each harmonising triad. A much more interesting and 'melodic' bass line can be shaped by using chord inversions and non-harmony notes to create a smoother part.

The two examples that follow both show the first four bars of *Twinkle Twinkle Little Star*. The bass line for the first example comprises the root notes of each of the chosen chords. In the second example, the bass line uses root notes, first inversions, passing notes, and also adds more harmonic movement in preparation for the cadence. As a result, the second version offers stylistic character and a smoother, more lyrical shape. See if you can describe the function of each note of the bass line in the second version as either a harmony note, passing note, or auxiliary note. (You could also try inventing an alternative bass line of your own.)

Twinkle Twinkle Litte Star

Twinkle Twinkle Litte Star

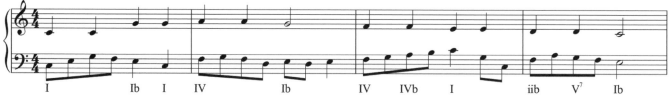

The example below shows the first eight bars of Minuet in G. As with the second version of *Twinkle Twinkle Little Star*, the melody for Minuet in G is supported by a well-shaped bass part that makes use of first-inversion chords and passing notes. However, you will notice that there is less movement in the bass line in Minuet in G, to help balance the faster quaver movement in the melody. In addition, note how the bass in bar 8 retains the quaver momentum at a point where the melody itself lacks rhythmic interest.

Petzold / J. S. Bach: Minuet in G

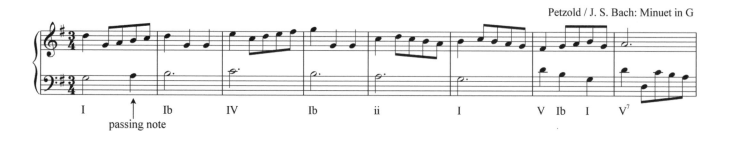

Exercise 7

This exercise will help you to gain practical experience of the sound and shape of well-constructed bass lines.

1. Choose an extract from *either* a classic popular song (such as Ben E. King's *Stand By Me* or *Penny Lane* by the Beatles) or a movement from a Baroque instrumental piece (a woodwind sonata, for example).

    ➢ Copy out the melody and bass part as accurately as possible (by hand or using notation software). Assign two appropriate instruments of your choice, for example, violin and cello or flute and bass guitar. Remember to think carefully about the issues involved if you choose to use a transposing instrument.

    ➢ Perform the piece, and listen to the strength of the two outer parts.

2. Working with a friend, play through some of the keyboard pieces in the *Notebook for Anna Magdalena Bach* by J. S. Bach. Take one hand each: one of you performing the melody; the other on the bass line. Many of these pieces are written for two parts only: Nos 4, 6, 7 and 18 are all good choices.

3. Sing or play through the soprano and bass parts only from some traditional hymn settings.

4. Play the outer parts from extracts of Baroque instrumental works. A good starting point would be to try some of the movements from Vivaldi's *Four Seasons* or the Bassoon Concerto in E minor.

In all of these exercises, notice how the bass parts are like melodies in their own right. Even though they generally have a larger number of wide leaps, they still create interesting lyrical shapes. It is possible to play many simple pieces with just the two outer parts (melody and bass); your 'inner ear' will fill in the harmonies even if they are not played.

Chord progressions

Certain ways of assembling chords in a sequence or progression found widespread acceptance over a period of music history and established the language of Western tonal harmony we are so familiar with today.

In general it is useful to think about:

> ➤ Chord progressions that lead up to a cadence point

> ➤ Commonly found sequences of chords between the start and end of phrases.

The two most important notes in a scale are the tonic and dominant notes; they are related to each other by the interval of a perfect 5th. Chords that relate to each other because their roots are a 5th apart form very strong chord progressions. This is why various combinations of chords ii, V and I work so well at cadences.

Here are some chord progressions that are frequently used to establish a perfect cadence:

1. In the first progression, the roots of the chords can be clearly seen, each spaced a 5th apart.

2. The root of chord ii in the lower octave gives the bass line a better shape. This demonstrates an important principle very well: that a rising 4th is effectively the same as a falling 5th.

3. By using the first inversion of chord ii the bass line achieves a smoother shape.

4. A common variation of the ii–V–I chord progression uses a second inversion of chord I immediately before the final two chords of a perfect cadence. (This progression is also described as a 'cadential 6-4'.)

Second inversion chords are also known as $^6_4$ chords because the upper notes are a 6th and 4th above the bass part. This method of indicating harmony, called **figured bass**, was used in the Baroque period.

Circle of 5ths

We can apply the principle that strong progressions have roots that fall in 5ths to longer chord sequences. If the roots of a chord progression keep moving down in perfect 5ths or up in perfect 4ths, a pattern known as a complete circle of 5ths is produced. Notice how all 12 notes of the chromatic scale are sounded before the circle returns to the starting pitch.

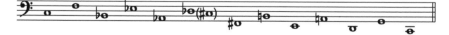

Notice how all 12 notes of the chromatic scale are sounded before the circle returns to the starting pitch (in this example, to the C an octave lower). To simplify the notation, the example changes from flats to sharps at D♭, which is the same sounding pitch as C♯.

Notes that sound the same but are written differently, such as C♯ and D♭, are called **enharmonic** equivalents.

In practice, in order to stay within a single key and provide a shorter route back to the tonic, composers prefer an abbreviated version of this progression, which is known as a **diatonic circle of 5ths**. Notice how the use of a falling diminished 5th is used between the subdominant and the leading note to achieve this:

Common progressions

Falling 5ths are not the only type of chord sequence that works well. Progressions where the roots fall in 3rds are also very strong and sound good; these are often combined with falling 5ths to create the following well-known chord patterns:

Exercise 8

Refer to your score of the first movement of Vivaldi's Bassoon Concerto in E minor.

1. Carefully follow the use of a circle of 5ths in the harmony of the section that features the solo bassoon and starts on the dominant (bars 50–53[2]). Notice that in the minor key the leading note is flattened by a semitone to create the shortened 'diatonic' version of the circle. (The circle is not quite complete by the time it reaches bar 53[2].)

2. In the tutti section that follows, beginning now on an E minor tonic at bar 53[3], the circle begins to mark out its route again. Follow the bass line and write out the complete cycle from E to E. Vivaldi is not just working to a formula: notice how he enhances the chord progression in bars 55–56 by incorporating suspended 7ths as trills, which alternate between the first and second violin parts.

Using second-inversion chords

Second-inversion chords tend to sound harmonically unstable, as if they want to move on to another chord. This is why a second inversion of chord I (Ic) often precedes a perfect cadence. In a **cadential 6-4** progression, chord Ic falls on the strong beat and the dominant root that follows forms the bass of both Ic and V. Sometimes the second of these repeated bass notes (chord V) drops down an octave, shown by the bracketed note in the next example. This creates the familiar shape shown in the bass part at the cadence:

J. Bishop, *Illsley*

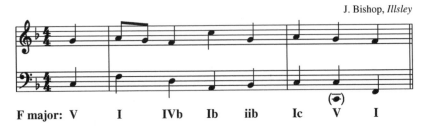

A second inversion can also be used when the music passes between the root position and first inversion of the same chord, as shown right. Incidentally, both of these progressions work equally well in reverse: Ib–Vc–I and IVb–Vc–IV. This type of second inversion always comes on the weaker part of the bar and is known as a passing $^6_4$.

G major: I Vc Ib   IVb Ic IV

Both types of second inversion, passing and cadential, appear in the following example – notice how smoothly the inner parts move:

Traditional, *All Through the Night*

G major: IVb Ic IV Ib IV Ic IVb vi ii ____ iib Ic _____ V I

Working in full texture

The music of *All Through the Night* (in the previous example), is written in a type of texture commonly found in four-part vocal writing. It is notated on two staves. The melody or soprano part is written on the treble stave with note stems pointing up. Below it is the alto part, written on the same treble stave but with stems pointing down. The tenor part is written on the bass stave with stems pointing up, below which comes the bass part with stems pointing down.

> For the purpose of these exercises, 'full texture' means at least three notes sounding together.

When writing in four-part harmony, at least one note in each triad has to appear twice in the chord in order to produce the required total of four parts. We speak of such notes as being doubled. There are some basic rules of good practice about which notes to double in a chord:

➤ The root is generally the best note to double. Alternatively, the 5th can be doubled (and is often the best option in second inversion chords).

➤ The 3rd of a major triad should not be doubled (doubling the 3rd in other triads is fine).

➤ A chord may contain the root in three of the four parts, as long as the 3rd of the chord is present in the remaining part.

When spacing chords in four-part harmony, note that:

➤ The interval between the soprano and alto, and between the alto and tenor, should never be more than an octave.

➤ The interval between the two lowest parts (tenor and bass) can be more than an octave.

A useful tip for achieving good spacing is to keep the tenor part high. Tenors are used to singing notes up to G above middle C, so don't be afraid to make use of leger lines above the bass stave when writing your tenor parts.

Exercise 9

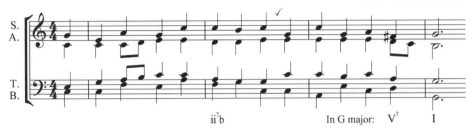

attrib. W Croft: *St Anne*

1. Sing or play through the soprano and bass parts. Notice that they are both more shapely and lyrical, compared to the supporting inner parts (alto and tenor).

2. Make a note of the key and mark in the ends of the phrases. Note that each phrase starts with a crotchet up-beat (anacrusis).

3. Sing the alto line alone. You will notice that it is quite static and avoids large leaps within each phrase.

4. Sing the tenor line alone. It is a little less static than the alto part, but in general avoids large leaps.

5. Indicate the harmonies using Roman numerals. Some chords have been provided for you.

6. Identify the cadences at the end of each phrase.

7. Analyse the relative movement between the soprano and bass parts, using the following descriptions:

   ➢ Contrary motion (moving in opposite directions)

   ➢ Parallel motion (moving in the same direction)

   ➢ Oblique motion (one part moves, the other part remains on the same note).

Voice leading

Singing, playing and analysing a piece of music written in this type of texture is a practical and more interesting way to identify the techniques of four-part harmony.

In traditional harmony, each part should be independent rather than shadowing each other. To help create independent parts, it is useful to consider certain types of movement or 'voice leading':

➢ The leading note has a natural pull upwards towards the tonic. In chord V, the 3rd of the chord is the leading note of the scale and so should rise to the tonic in that part

➢ When using chord V^7, not only should the leading note rise to the tonic, but whichever part has the 7th should fall by step to a note of the next chord, as shown in the cadence at the end of the example used in Exercise 9

➢ Avoiding moving in parallel intervals (consecutives) of unison, octaves or perfect 5ths between parts, as this type of movement is considered to be weak because the parts do not sound truly independent of each other.

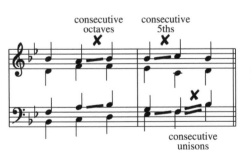

➢ In the example used in Exercise 9, notice how in bar 2^1 the 7th note of chord ii^{7}b in the soprano is prepared in the same part in the preceding chord (the C, which is a 3rd in the A minor chord in bar 1^4).

Traditional rules of harmony state that the 3rd of a major chord should not be doubled, but the 3rd of a minor chord can be doubled. You will notice, however, in bar 1^3 of the example used in Exercise 9, the 3rd of the tonic chord is sounded twice in the alto and bass parts. This is a good example of how a breaking of the 'rule' can be justified on the grounds of a better musical outcome. One solution would have been to put a middle C in the alto part. However, that would have created parallel 5ths between the soprano and alto in bar 1^{2-3}.

Doubling

Here are two workings of the third and fourth phrases of the hymn melody used in Exercise 9.

Comparing two solutions

Example 1

attrib. W Croft: *St Anne*

In this first example, bar 1^4 avoids doubling the 3rd of the G major chord, however it creates an awkward leap up to the E in the tenor part. The passing-note phrase in the tenor line of bar 2 appears musical, however it creates parallel 5ths between the tenor and bass from beats 2–3 (the parallel 5ths are identified by grey noteheads).

Example 2

attrib. W Croft: *St Anne*

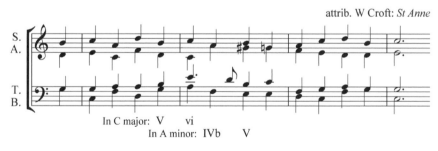

In the second example, the doubling of the 3rd in chord V (bar 1^4) allows for a more satisfying shape in the tenor line. The E sounds first as the 5th degree of chord vi; it then becomes a suspension (bar 2^2), prepared on 2^1 and then resolving to become the root of chord IVb, before approaching the imperfect cadence in A minor on beat 3. The overlapping of parts between tenor and alto is entirely justified on the grounds of a 'musical' solution. Alternatively, it would also be possible to put the tenor line in the alto part, but be careful to avoid creating parallel 5ths as you move from V to vi – a common mistake!

Part writing: summary It is good practice to try to conform to the rules of part writing wherever you can. However, as the examples above show, the most important priority is the lyrical shaping of each vocal line.

It is useful to note that these 'rules' about parallel intervals apply to traditional part-writing. Consecutive parallel octaves are frequently used in piano and orchestral music, and parallel root-position triads (which generate parallel 5ths) are common in modern pop music.

In your coursework exercises you should show an understanding of the way that inner parts connect from one beat to the next, whether the harmony is moving in block chords or in a more linear, melodic style. It is particularly important to observe voice-leading conventions if you choose to submit hymn-melody harmonisations.

Exercise 10

This exercise uses a traditional melody, with an opening harmonisation given on the guitar. A full texture for a polyphonic instrument such as the guitar should distinguish in the notation between the bass part (stems down) and the inner harmony, using idiomatically notated chords. Complete the remaining three bars.

Traditional English: *The Miller of Dee*

A complete exercise

This chapter has covered a range of starting points for your exercises. Bearing in mind the list of options mentioned on page 23, the following completed exercise is only one example of many possibilities. The given material is the complete melody plus the whole of the four-bar introduction. The actual working is 16 bars long and is modelled on the three-part texture of the given opening:

Name ....
Date ....

The Ash Grove

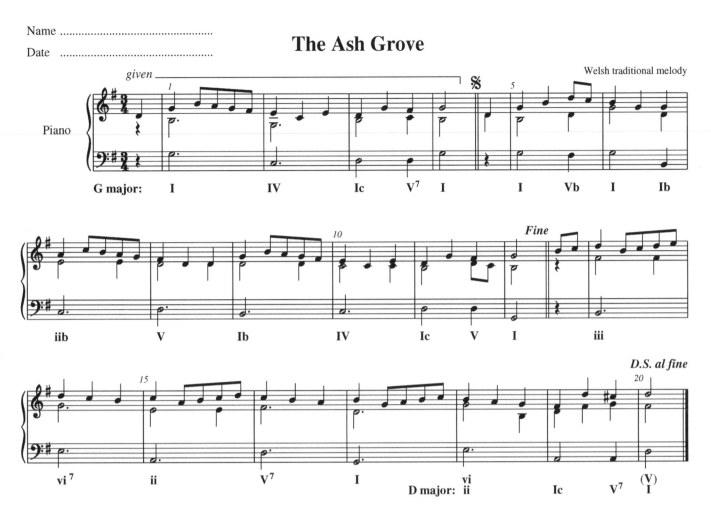

The instruction *D.S. al fine* at bar 20 tells the performer to repeat the music from the sign 𝄋 until the word *Fine* in bar 12.

Notice how the bass and chords follow the descending sequence of the melody from bar 13, not deviating from the pattern until bar 18.

Modulation

There is a **modulation** (change of key) to the dominant (D major) in bars 19–20 of the exercise above, signalled by C♯ in the melody and confirmed by a perfect cadence in the new key.

The E-minor triad in bar 18 prepares the way for this modulation by acting as a **pivot chord** – a chord that is common to two keys. Here, E minor is chord vi of G major, the key we are leaving, and chord ii of D major, the key we are approaching. Notice how the modulation is shown in the chord symbols. These make it clear how the music has moved from one key to another and how the chord in bar 18 acts as a pivot chord.

You should include at least one or two exercises in your portfolio that show you know how to modulate. Modulations are likely to be to closely related keys, such as the dominant, subdominant or relative minor.

You will need a second modulation in order to return to the tonic. Here, the chord in bar 20 is chord I of D major, but also chord V of G major. It thus prepares the way for the return of the tonic key when the music repeats from bar 5.

In the first movement of Beethoven's Violin Concerto in D, Op. 61, examine some of the different ways the composer modulates to a new key:

➤ Bar 50: following a passage in D major, the cadence ends with the tonic chord in all instruments (bar 50^1); the dominant note (A) at 50^{2-4} acts as a simple link to an immediate D minor chord at the start of bar 51.

➤ Bar 465: the composer moves from D major to the subdominant key of G major in the space of three bars. Write Roman numerals beneath the chords in bars 465–466. The E minor chord at the start of bar 467 can be described as either chord ii in D major or chord vi in G major. It is the pivot point at which the former key gives way to the new one established by the perfect cadence that follows in bars 467–468.

An exercise completed under timed conditions

Towards the end of the course you will complete an exercise without help from your teacher and under supervised conditions. You will be given an hour to do this and you will be able to use an instrument such as a keyboard, guitar or notation software (with any assistance disabled) as you work.

Assessment

Of the 45 marks available for your portfolio:

➤ 20 are awarded for harmonic language (your choice and pacing of chords, and use of effective progressions)

➤ 15 are awarded for technique (creating a strong and well-shaped bass line, continuing the texture from a given opening, identifying and providing the correct working for key changes, and a clear understanding of voice-leading)

➤ 10 are awarded for the clear and accurate use of notation.

The exercise on the previous page should achieve a good mark because:

➤ The bass has a strong shape resulting from the use of primary triads in root position, along with occasional secondary triads and inversions

➤ The inner part moves smoothly, avoiding awkward intervals, and the bass moves largely in contrary motion to the melody

➤ The chord progressions lead effectively to the cadences and include correctly resolved dominant 7ths, appropriate use of chord Ic, modulation and (in bars 13–17) a falling-5ths pattern in which a harmonic sequence (iii–vi^7–ii–V^7) nicely reflects the melodic sequence in bars 13–16

➤ The work has been checked for good voice-leading, with no consecutive (parallel) 5ths or octaves between melody and bass.

Maintaining momentum and a sense of harmonic direction from the start to the end of each phrase is especially important. With experience and observation of how harmony functions in your set works, you will become more confident and successful in the harmonic choices you make.

Preparing your portfolio

Exercises may be either hand-written, providing they are legible and accurate, or you may use notation software. As this is a coursework unit, the moderator will expect to see your teacher's marks and comments on your work. This helps the moderator to understand the way you have been taught and the understanding you have gained throughout the course. It is often better not to produce neat copies since new mistakes easily creep in when making changes.

Make sure that the given material is clearly identified in each exercise, so that the moderator can see exactly what you have added. Use a highlighter pen or provide a copy of the original template you were given for each exercise.

Remember that it is possible to make mistakes even when using a computer notation programme. Notes of chords in each part must be vertically aligned and notes must have correct accidentals – for example, writing A♭ rather than G♯ is an error if you are in the key of A minor. Correct beaming of grouped notes is also important.

All exercises must include chord symbols – either Roman numerals (with inversion letters) to show the chords, or letter names (with slash chords to show inversions) or figured bass. You should not use guitar tab because this shows finger positions rather than actual pitches, but you can add tab above the stave notation if you find it useful when trying out your work.

Your teacher will assess your portfolio and it will then need to be available for moderation if required. It should be clear to the moderator which of your exercises form the core evidence upon which assessment has been made. It is not necessary for you to include preliminary work. Make sure that access to your exercises is easy; a simple paper clip to group your sheets together is more effective than plastic pockets.

The following checklist can help you make sure that when you select the exercises to include in your portfolio, all requirements for Section A of the composing unit have been met.

Portfolio checklist

☐ At least six exercises completed during the course

☐ One further exercise completed under supervision towards the end of the course

☐ All exercises contain between eight and 24 bars of added material

☐ Bass line and chord symbols completed in all exercises

☐ Bass line, chord symbols *and inner part(s)* completed in at least two full-texture exercises

☐ A range of keys represented, with at least one exercise in a minor key

☐ Appropriate identification of cadences and cadence approaches

☐ Examples that show the appropriate use (and resolution) of chords V^7 and ii^7

☐ Examples showing the appropriate use of second inversions

☐ Example(s) including modulation

☐ Notation checked for accuracy and legibility

Section B: Instrumental Techniques

For this part of the unit you can write *either*:

➢ A composition for 4–10 instruments or

➢ An arrangement of a lead sheet for 4–10 instruments.

Whichever you choose, you will need to submit a full score of your work in staff notation, a commentary and a recording. If you choose the arrangement option, you must also submit the original lead sheet that you used.

Although most of the following information refers to composing, much of it also applies to arranging. Your work will be judged by the same criteria whichever option you choose. Some specific issues that affect arrangements are discussed on page 58.

Introduction

The area of study, The Expressive Use of Instrumental Techniques, takes centre stage in this part of the composing unit. You will need to understand the characteristics of a range of instruments and the ways in which they can be combined. Your own experience as a performer and your knowledge of the set works will form a good starting point for this. The word 'expressive' in the area of study is of particular importance – in composing we express our thoughts and feelings, sometimes in a surprisingly objective and methodical way, via the medium of a musical instrument. To express is to *communicate*. You must have your audience in mind, if you want to be really successful in communicating your compostitional ideas to potential listeners.

The composition must be for 4–10 instruments, which can be acoustic, amplified or a combination of both. You can include voices if you wish, but only in addition to the 4–10 instruments, and you should note that you can only gain credit for your writing for instruments.

You have a wide choice of instruments (but see right for some important exceptions). However, it makes sense to write for:

➢ A group of fellow students who will be available to try out your work as it progresses, and to rehearse and perform it for the final recording

➢ A group of instruments that will sound well together.

The upper limit is three minutes, but there is no penalty if your work does not precisely meet this requirement. You should aim to say everything you want to say, musically speaking, within this time. Be disciplined and avoid rambling on for longer than necessary, but avoid a piece that is too short as it won't allow you to show the full value of your ideas and range of expertise.

You can write in any style you wish, but it is easier to work in an idiom with which you are really familiar. All composers have learned from existing music by playing it, listening to it, studying it and arranging it, only gradually developing their own composing voice. It is important that you too study the music of others as a way of developing your own skill as a composer. In the commentary it is especially important to give details of all the pieces you have studied that are relevant to your composition, and explain precisely how they have informed your work.

Aural familiarity with a range of musical ideas in the work of others is likely to show clearly in your composition, but it needs carefully documenting in the commentary too. As you study the scores and recordings of the prescribed works, you will have the opportunity to learn a great deal about the composer's craft in both a classical and jazz context through the analysis of specific pieces. In addition, music that has been an important part of your life experience to date may be significant in the shaping of your ideas.

➢ Think about the music that you know – which styles do you like and know well, what gaps are there in your current listening experiences?

➢ Borrow scores of your favourite pieces from your college, school or local library (or, if available, download them from the internet). Identify and copy out the melodies, short motifs, rhythms or chord progressions that you find particularly interesting. Keep a journal of your musical discoveries.

Which instruments can I use?

You need to show that you can write for instruments, not their synthesised equivalents. For example, a flute part should be designed to be played on a flute, not a synthesiser. However, you are allowed to use synthetic sounds in the final recording, if necessary. If you and your teacher are unsure what is permissible, contact OCR and ask.

How long should the piece be?

Style

Aural familiarity

International Music Score Library Project (http://imslp.org) is a useful source of public music. Scores, however, may not always be accurate.

➤ Take stock of your current repertoire as a performer. Discuss the range of music available for your instrument or voice with your specialist teacher if you have one.

➤ Do you play in an ensemble? Is the music that you play relevant to your composing ideas? Consider forming a group to experiment with composing ideas or to perform arrangements of interesting music.

What will be examined? The 45 marks available for your composition or arrangement are split into four categories, each of which will be explored in detail over the following pages:

➤ **Materials (10 marks)** are your basic ideas, the building blocks of your piece such as rhythmic patterns, melodies, bass parts and chord progressions, together with a clear account in your commentary of the listening that has influenced the shaping of these materials

➤ **Use of medium (15 marks)** refers to your understanding of the particular qualities of the instruments you have used and the ways in which you have combined them

➤ **Technique (10 marks)** is the skill with which your materials have been constructed on a small scale and then developed, combined and connected to form a larger structure

➤ **Communication (10 marks)** is the way in which you have conveyed your ideas in both the score (which needs to be complete and accurate) and the recording (which needs to give an effective interpretation/performance of your music).

As there is no restriction on the style of your work, remember that the examples given in the rest of this chapter indicate only some of the possibilities open to you.

Materials

Melodic materials

One of the most important elements in many types of music is melody. Your work in Section A of this unit will help you to understand the various ways in which melodies can be constructed. The melodies you are using will be by established composers; as you perform them, they will provide you with good models of small-scale structure. The character of a melody is shaped by its rhythm, pitches, overall contour and pace. Strong melodies often consist of mainly stepwise movement with occasional leaps. Think about the opening of the well-known tune *Greensleeves* – the melodic intervals reflect this basic principle and we can also hear that the leaps are ones with strong harmonic implications (chord notes are marked *):

The linear intervals created as a melody moves from one note to the next can have a profound effect on its character. John Williams'

theme for *Schindler's List* is deeply expressive whether or not we know the subject matter of the film. Another melody, Beethoven's *Ode to Joy* has a somewhat measured and noble quality. Consider the extent to which these characteristics are related to the use of stepwise and angular movement within the melodies.

Both pitch and rhythm play a part in determining the character of a melody as can be heard in Henry Mancini's *Pink Panther* theme:

Even when melodies are not particularly distinctive in either pitch or rhythm, we can see invention in the way they unfold. Notice how the melody of the folk song *The Water is Wide* (below) slowly expands the range of notes outlined in each of its four phrases. There is a firm sense of upward direction in the unfolding melody as it moves toward the high point at bar 9 before finally coming to rest in the fourth phrase:

The climax of a melody is often found between two-thirds and three-quarters of the way through, as in the example below. It doesn't have to be loud, highpitched and joyous – it could be low, quiet and mysterious.

A good way to write a melody is to start with a short, memorable **motif** which can be repeated, manipulated or contrasted to form a phrase. More importantly, such motifs can become a source for development in different ways later in the piece.

A short motif can exert a powerful presence: think about the opening of Beethoven's Symphony No. 5 or the timpani motif in the first bar of his Violin Concerto; equally, consider the melodic fragments from which an entire fabric can be woven in the work of composers such as Steve Reich, Michael Nyman and Stephen Sondheim.

The next example is built on a four-note motif. When the motif is repeated, its opening interval (an octave) contracts to a 7th. The second half of the phrase starts with another repetition of the motif (in which the opening interval is now reduced to a 5th), but this time the motif is extended to eight crotchet beats in length, thus balancing the combined length of its first two appearances. The graph-like lines above the stave show the contour of the melody, which consists of a long descent to balance the upward leaps at the start of the motif:

[Allegro]   Bach, Orchestral Suite No. 3 in D, Gavotte I

Exercise 12

1. Construct a balanced melody of four phrases in an inverted arch shape (⌣) in which the lowest point is reached in the third phrase. Base it on a short motif that is modified and then extended to provide contrast. The previous two music examples are good models of this.

2. In your study of the set works, you will notice that composers frequently shape themes out of predominantly stepwise movement. Compare the opening eight-bar string melody in the fourth movement of Haydn's Symphony No. 103 in E♭ with the oboe melody at the start of Beethoven's Violin Concerto in D. What gives character to the melodies?

3. Duke Ellington's *Koko* is written in a transposed aeolian mode. Find out about other modes such as dorian and phrygian or those of other cultures – Arabic or Balinese, for example. Write out some melodic ideas using these various pitch patterns.

4. Investigate the ways in which motifs are used and distinctive themes constructed in as many of the following works as possible:

   ➤ Delius: 'La Calinda' from *Three Orchestral Pieces*

   ➤ Bizet: 'Farandole' from *L'Arlésienne* Suite No. 2

   ➤ Grieg: 'Morning Mood' and 'In the Hall of the Mountain King' from *Peer Gynt* Suite

   ➤ Bartók: Concerto for Orchestra, third movement

   ➤ Reich: Three Movements for Orchestra (1986), second movement.

Bass materials

We have already noted in Section A (page 31) that bass notes underpin the harmonic possibilities of a piece of music. A bass part may have a strongly melodic character, as found in music of a **contrapuntal** texture where each of the voices has an independent line. In rock music, **riffs** in the bass part can play an important role too; they may be the foundation upon which an entire piece is built.

A **ground bass** is a repeating bass part above which different melodies unfold. While it is a device often associated with Baroque music, it can be very effective in other styles of music. Pachelbel's well-known Canon in D is built upon a simple ground bass that is played 28 times, while a series of increasingly complex melodies unfold in canon above it. Other examples to study include the Ricercare from Bach's *Musical Offering*, Britten's Passacaglia from *Peter Grimes* and *When God Created the Coffee Break* from the album *Strange Place for Snow* by the Esbjörn Svensson Trio.

Your study of jazz recordings will allow you to investigate a range of bass lines and their relationship to the harmonic framework. You may have studied the 12-bar blues for GCSE and now at AS level you will learn how standard bass patterns can be presented in various interesting ways to suit 8-, 16-, 20- and 32-bar structures.

A weakness in many AS compositions is a bass part that doesn't go beyond simply reinforcing the harmony and so lacks real interest in its own right. Yet, in an iconic work like Miles Davis' *So What*, the bass player is entrusted with the most important motivic material from the start. In addition to the good practice you will find in the orchestral scores and jazz recordings you study, the music of the following bass players may be instructive:

Clearly notated examples of typical walking, rock and Latin bass lines can be found in the Appendix of *Jazz Styles: History and Analysis* by Mark C. Gridley. Prentice Hall, 1978/2008, ISBN 978-0-136005-89-6.

➢ Jack Bruce (Cream)

➢ Jaco Pastorius (Weather Report and solo)

➢ Michael 'Flea' Balzary (Red Hot Chili Peppers)

➢ Victor Wooten.

Exercise 13

Take time to look at the detail in the bass part of Duke Ellington's *Koko*, in order to understand the variety of ways a walking bass can be expressed. Find examples of broken chord outlines and their inversions, stepwise movement, use of two alternating notes and chromatic fills. How does Ellington ensure Jimmy Blanton's solo moments are heard and how are they given rhythmic prominence?

Rhythmic materials

Rhythm is a key ingredient in establishing the character of a piece. Steady crotchets, robotic quavers, lilting triplets, snappy dotted rhythms, lively syncopations, rapid semiquavers or asymmetric patterns such as those created by the heavy string accents in Stravinsky's *Rite of Spring* – each can create a different mood.

Dance-based music is usually associated with particular rhythmic patterns and regular phrase lengths: slow duple time for stately pavans, fast compound time for jigs, moderate triple time for waltzes, duple-time phrases that begin halfway through the bar for gavottes (as in the example on page 45) and so on.

The Latin music associated with the countries of South America has enjoyed great popularity in a variety of musical contexts. For example, several of the numbers in Bernstein's *West Side Story* (1957) are based on Latin-American dances. Such influences have been heard in popular music and jazz for many decades. More recently, the work of the Cuban ensemble *Buena Vista Social Club* contributed to a revival of interest in Latin-American music. The continuing success of artists such as Gloria Estefan and Carlos Santana (who released *Supernatural* – the hugely successful album produced in collaboration with younger artists) is convincing proof that its popularity continues.

African drumming and Balinese gamelan as well as the music of the medieval French composer Pérotin have influenced the music of Steve Reich. The compositions of Philip Glass and Peter Gabriel's film scores similarly show the rhythmic influences of other times and cultures. The short works listed right provide further fruitful opportunities to experience ostinati and driving rhythms at work.

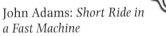

John Adams: *Short Ride in a Fast Machine*

Louis Andriessen: Instrumental III from *M is for Man, Music, Mozart*

Graham Fitkin: *Servant*

Remember that your initial rhythmic ideas will need refinement and control as you continue to work on your composition.

It can be productive to consider: working with more unusual time signatures; composing using a changing pulse; subdividing the pulse into unpredictable rhythmic groupings. The following works provide excellent examples to listen to:

➢ The waltz-like second movement in $\frac{5}{4}$ of Tchaikovsky's Symphony No. 6 in B minor

➢ *Take Five* written in $\frac{5}{4}$ time and *Unsquare Dance* in $\frac{7}{4}$ time, both performed by The Dave Brubeck Quartet

➢ The subdivisions within the crotchet pulse of Radiohead's *Pyramid Song*

➢ Bulgarian Rhythm (113, 115), from Bartók's *Mikrokosmos* Vol. IV for Solo Piano.

Harmonic materials

If you write in a tonal idiom you will have a feast of listening materials on which to draw, including and beyond the set works. But there are other ways to organise pitch such as serial or nonserial atonality and modality. Most popular music is either tonal or modal, and so beginning with a chord progression is often a good starting point for many student composers.

Listen to Barber's *Adagio for Strings* and excerpts from Michael Nyman's film scores for examples in which the harmonic materials dominate the musical content. For both these composers, the richness of their harmonic language is influenced by music of the Baroque and Classical periods. Nyman openly acknowledges his borrowings from Purcell and Mozart.

You will learn in your study of the set works how the organisation of pitch is closely connected with the musical structure. The keys or tonal centres often provide an important means of defining a section, which may move on to develop initial ideas or provide a complete contrast.

Exercise 14

1. Research some characteristic rhythms of dance music from a different culture. Compose a short piece of 16–20 bars for two instruments that incorporate your findings.

2. Listen to extracts from Nyman's 'Chasing sheep is best left to shepherds' (from *The Draughtsman's Contract*) or Overture and Serenata from Stravinsky's *Pulcinella*. In these works, both composers write in a pastiche Baroque style but with a modern sound.

3. Use the harmonic outline of the first four bars of Vivaldi's Bassoon Concerto in E minor (given below) to create your own harmonic texture for a section of wind instruments. Extend this sequence harmonically for a further four bars.

Em	Am	B^7	Em
Em	C	Am/C	B^7

4. Compose a short chord sequence of your own for keyboard or guitar using a single harmonic figuration. Create a complementary melody for an instrument of your choice.

Use of medium

Marks in this category are awarded for how well you have written for the instruments you have used – are the parts playable and do they exploit the character of the instrument? Is there interest in all of the parts – or are some condemned to dull accompaniment patterns with little melodic interest?

In preparation, you will need to research all you can about the instruments you use. Discuss with the performers: the various tone colours available at different dynamics; any special effects that might be possible; how much time is needed to insert a mute or take a breath on a wind instrument; which chords are possible on a guitar; which musical features (such as glissandos, trills or fast passages involving low notes) might prove difficult; what different types of tonguing, bowing or vibrato sound like, and so on.

Will your composition be written for a small group of soloists: a brass quartet; a string quartet with saxophone or electric guitar, for example? Or you may wish to compose for a small chamber orchestra – a string section with wind soloists or tuned percussion perhaps. In your composition for between four and ten instruments, note the following: a section of violins counts as 'one part'; a full string section as 'four parts'; and you should make your intentions clear in your commentary.

The best way to learn the skills of **orchestration** – how to compose for different instruments – is to study and get to know plenty of scores.

You will be taking a detailed look at violin writing from both a solo and orchestral perspective in the study of your prescribed works. We have used the violin in the following section as an example of the type of research you could usefully undertake in preparation for writing a composition. Similar principles covered here will apply to investigating any instrument.

Even though we are used to hearing synthesised strings in popular and ambient music, for the purposes of this unit it is the original acoustic instrument that you should have in mind. If you are used to composing at a keyboard or computer, a common mistake is to write parts that are 'pianistic' but unsuitable or even impossible for a string instrument to play.

Writing for violin

The violin is considered one of the most expressive of instruments and has inspired a treasury of music from composers across the centuries. It has a range of more than three and a half octaves, but there is much more to take into account than just the lowest and highest notes. If you are to write well for this instrument, it is worth taking time to learn about the open strings (which are tuned in perfect 5ths) and the relative placement of the fingers on the strings in various positions.

First position fingering for all the 'natural' notes on the violin:

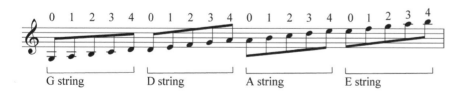

The widely spaced arpeggiated accompaniment figure in bar 1 of Vivaldi's Bassoon Concerto in E minor is less demanding than it first appears, when considered in the context of finger placement on the first violin:

The figuration in the first half of the bar outlines an E minor chord. The four notes are played as follows:

➢ G string: open. D string: 1st finger. A string: 1st finger. D string: 1st finger.

The figuration in the second half of the bar outlines an A minor chord. The four notes are played as follows:

➢ G string: 1st finger. D string: 1st finger. A string: 2nd finger. D string: 1st finger.

Each string has its own timbre or sound quality. Ask a friend to play the open strings for you. Notice that they have a broader, fuller sound than a 'stopped note'; open-string notes cannot be adjusted in pitch or treated with vibrato. For this reason players will avoid playing an open string in the middle of a melodic line, choosing a 'stopped' version of the note instead, as the performer has more control over the sound.

> **Vibrato:** The left-hand finger stopping the note oscillates to produce a slight variation in pitch. Performers reserve intense vibrato for the most expressive moments, but sometimes play without vibrato if a more remote, emotionally detached sound is required.

There are two basic means of sound production on the violin – bowed (arco) and plucked (pizzicato). The instrument is extremely versatile and has a wide range of possibilities in the context of both rapid passages and longer expressive lines.

It is useful to have a basic understanding of the principles of bowing techniques. The down-bow movement produces a strong start to the note, the up-bow less so. String players sometimes write down- (⊓) or up-bow (∨) symbols on their music to indicate the required bow movement. As they gain experience this becomes less necessary.

Slurs and phrase marks are some of the most important ways of indicating the bowing requirements for string players. A slur indicates the number of notes to be played in a single bow stroke. These markings show how to 'articulate' the music – for a wind player it is by the use of the tongue; for a string player, a similar effect is achieved by control of the bow. The violin is capable of playing more than one note at a time; 'double stopping' or even four-note chords are possible, and there are many examples for you to study in the prescribed works.

The violin as soloist

The violin has three main conventional roles: as a soloist, a member of a chamber ensemble (e.g. string quartet), and an orchestral player.

The solo violin has a 'singing' quality that can be assertive and intense, reflective or intimate, and is able to balance well within the mix of other instrumentalists.

Here are some of the idiomatic characteristics of the solo violin as displayed in Beethoven's Violin Concerto in D, Op. 61:

➢ **Agility and penetrating clarity in the upper register:** note how the soloist climbs effortlessly into the stratosphere from bar 91, to play an octave higher than the oboe melody at bar 102.

➢ **Warmth of the lower register:** after the virtuosity of the cadenza the soloist plays the second theme with the orchestra for the first time, in a contrasting lower register in bar 511.

➢ **Scalic movement:** the twists and turns of semiquaver scalic movement couched within a variety of rhythmical groupings are characteristic of the instrument in bars 217–224, for example.

➢ **Arpeggio figuration**: the composer covers a wide pitch range within a single bar at bar 111.

➢ **Decorative potential**: the exposed semiquaver decoration of the cadence at bars 116–117.

➢ **Embellishment**: note the textural variation possibilities – the violin embellishes the simple ascending scale motif (first heard in bar 18) with octaves, turns, scalic movement by step and in 3rds, as the soloist dominates the ensemble from bar 126.

➢ **The trill**: in the hands of an accomplished string player it is a particularly effective ornament. Violins are able to vigorously sustain their output over long periods, without the breath constraints made on the stamina of wind players. Note the effectiveness of the melodic material in the woodwind at bar 143 against the violin's trill, and the return of the rhythm motif beneath the chromatically ascending trill sequence from bar 205.

A violinist in an orchestra takes on a more formal role within the body of a larger group of players. A chamber ensemble or quartet allows for a team approach but with more scope for individuality than in an orchestra.

The violin within an ensemble

While the string section can be thought of as a choir of voices, writing chordally for the section is only one of several options. It is instructive to examine the scoring of the string textures in the fourth movement of the Haydn Symphony No. 103 in E♭:

Paired entries	
bars 9–12	Vln 1 + Vln 2 function together as do Vla + Vc + Cb in imitative response.

Imitation	
bars 220–224	Vln 1 entry is answered by Vc + Cb four bars later (at bar 224).

An idiomatic string texture	
bar 99	Strings play with a homophonic quaver texture that adds density, pace and weight in support of the *fortissimo* dynamic marking (bar 101), while the woodwind section sustains the chords.
bars 133, 141, 310, 349	Compare the groupings, doublings and rhythmic variety of the string parts at these points in the music.

Doubling with other instruments	
bar 76	Lower strings are doubled by the bassoons.
bar 86	Evaluate the doublings of the orchestral chord, and note which parts have rhythmic interest and which remain static.
bar 91	Fl combines with Vln 1.
bar 172	Cl shares in the expression of the repeated note motif with Vln 2 + lower strings.

Exercise 15

1. In the first movement of Beethoven's Violin Concerto in D, identify one section of music in the solo violin part that must be played entirely on the highest string, E, and one section that exploits the richness of the lower string timbre.

2. Study bars 438^3–452^1 of the solo violin part with its range of articulation, slurs and broader phrase markings. Think through (or mime) the up-bow and down-bow strokes that a performer would use.

3. Listen to two different recordings to compare the performance interpretation of bowing and articulation.

String quartet listening

Further listening suggestions

'Dodge The Dodo' from *Love Is Real* by Ulf Wakenius. Listen to the way the first violin takes the role of the drum kit in this arrangement.

A great many 'extended' string techniques associated with avant-garde music can be heard in works such as Penderecki's *Threnody to the Victims of Hiroshima* and George Crumb's *Black Angels*. You may wish to make use of them in an appropriate stylistic context, but don't forget that more standard techniques can offer a huge amount of variety.

In addition to the body of Classical quartets written by Haydn and Mozart, there are many compositional discoveries to be made in each of the quartets composed in the early 20th century by Ravel and Debussy, and the group of six quartets composed by Bartók.

Techniques demonstrated in these works include: *con sordini* (play 'with the mute'); the use of harmonics, tremolo between non-adjacent notes, various bowing sonorities such as *sul ponticello* (play 'near the bridge') and *col legno* (play 'with the wood' of the bow), in addition to extreme pizzicato techniques such as snapping the string against the fingerboard. The pizzicato chords of the second movement of Debussy's String Quartet in G minor (alternating with the quasi-Spanish melodic line) produce a stylised guitar effect.

Orchestral Technique: A Manual for Students by Gordon Jacob. Oxford University Press, 1931/1982, ISBN 978-0-193182-04-2.

Orchestration by Cecil Forsyth. Dover Publications, 1914/1986, ISBN 978-0-486243-83-2.

Orchestration by Walter Piston. W. W. Norton, 1955, ISBN 978-0-393097-40-5.

Rock, Jazz and Pop Arranging by Daryl Runswick. Faber Music, 1993, ISBN 978-0-571511-08-2.

When researching the capabilities of the instruments you intend to use, remember that there are many sources of advice:

➤ The performers you are going to use and any specialist tutors who may teach in your school or college

➤ The classical and jazz set works you are studying, which include many examples of good practice

➤ Books such as those listed left

➤ Internet sites, such as www.bbc.co.uk/orchestras/guide/, www.soundjunction.org ('instruments and voices' section) and www.nyphilkids.org ('instrument storage room' section) – the last of these is aimed at children but all three include detailed examples and useful factual information.

Exercise 16

Undertake a thorough investigation of an instrument you would like to include in your composition. Use a range of resources including books, scores and the internet; be sure to listen to some of the music that will be recommended in the sources you use. Prepare a five-minute presentation for other students, including a practical demonstration if you have researched an instrument that you play yourself.

Technique

Marks for technique are awarded for small-scale structures (the way that phrases are organised) and for the form of the entire composition. In both cases, the key to success is to balance unity with variety – too many new or unconnected ideas and your piece will not seem integrated; too much repetition and it risks becoming predictable and boring.

Small-scale structure

The single repeated notes – found in the opening of the fourth movement of Haydn's Symphony No. 103 (bar 5, first violin, E♭s) and the opening of the first movement of Beethoven's Violin Concerto in D major (bar 1, timpani, Ds) – are developed thematically in both works. You will know that it is a composition tool to build melodies from short, balanced units often two or four bars in length. Such motifs are balanced because they are of equal length and are often arranged in complementary pairs (questions and answers).

In the first movement of the E minor Bassoon Concerto, Vivaldi presents an opening melodic phrase that contains the 'seeds' from which the music grows. The music example below shows the opening melody, played by the second violin, up to bar 9.

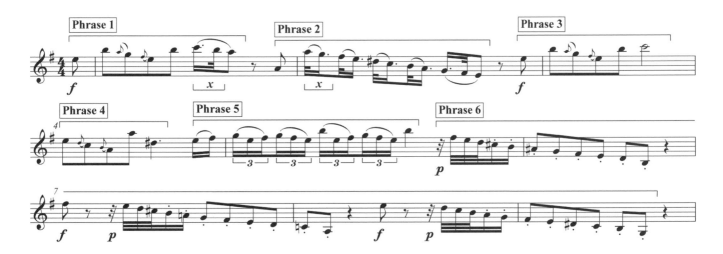

The anacrusis is a unifying idea that Vivaldi uses for many of his melodic phrases. The first three phrases start with a quaver, the fourth has no up-beat, semiquavers start the fifth phrase, followed by a still more elaborately constructed anacrusis for the sixth phrase. This 'varying' of the same idea is a technique Vivaldi uses to unify while avoiding precise repetition.

Refer to the music example on the previous page as you read the following analysis of the opening 13 bars of the melody played by the second violin:

➤ **Phrase 1** (bars 0⁴–1³) is built around the broken-chord shape and its ending contains the rhythmic seed of the next phrase (ref. brackets 'x').

➤ **Phrase 2** (bars 1⁴–2³) is a descending minor scale response using the dotted rhythm of phrase 1 but now reversed (ref. brackets 'x').

➤ **Phrase 3** (bars 2⁴–3) repeats phrase 1 but with a held C minim on beat 3.

➤ **Phrase 4** (bar 4–4³) surprises us with a transposed version of the broken-chord figure, but without an opening anacrusis.

➤ **Phrase 5** (bars 4⁴–5³) elaborates the tonic chord with decorative semiquavers that build towards a crotchet B on beat 3.

➤ **Phrase 6** (bars 5⁴–9) uses the descending scale idea from phrase 2, but is rhythmically developed to use a faster straight pattern of demisemiquaver, semiquavers and quavers. This pattern is played three times in a descending harmonic sequence, using a strong unison and octave texture.

It is worth studying the variations used around the melodic and harmonic minor scale throughout the first movement. While balanced phrasing is a typical characteristic of music from the Classical period, the concept of creating a melody by building on what has gone before is an excellent way of balancing unity with variety. This can be applied to many different styles of music.

Exercise 17

Evaluate the small-scale structure of some melodies you are working with in Section A of the composing unit and of some of the melodies you play in your favourite pieces.

Developing ideas Creating music from a few tiny melodic cells can be one of the most fruitful ways of composing, since they offer the potential for development in all sorts of ways, both later in the phrase and later in the piece. Composers have often used standard techniques to enable a melodic idea to grow from the briefest of starting points. Motifs are often repeated before being transformed in some way. Possible transformations include:

Transposition	Moving the motif uniformly to a new key
Tonal sequence	Repeating the motif at a higher or lower pitch but adapting intervals to stay in the same key
Interval alteration	Keeping the general shape but reducing or enlarging the size of some intervals
Fragmentation	Using just part of the motif
Extension	Continuing the motif beyond its previous end
Decoration	Replacing notes with several shorter notes
Simplification	Replacing several short notes with a single long note
Inversion	Reversing the direction of all the intervals: e.g. rising 3rds become falling 3rds
Augmentation	Systematically increasing the length of notes
Diminution	Systematically reducing the length of notes

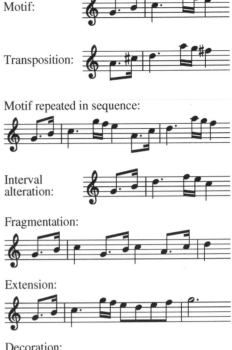

Other techniques include retrograde, in which the order of the notes is reversed (so G–B–C–G–F–E becomes E–F–G–C–B–G) and retrograde inversion, in which the notes of the retrograde version are also inverted. However, these types of transformation are not easily perceived by the listener, and tend to be used mainly in particular styles of music such as serialism and sometimes minimalism.

Composers frequently combine different types of transformation – so a motif might be fragmented and then that fragment might be used in sequence, inverted and decorated.

What this all boils down to is that you really don't need many ideas for a well-integrated composition – it is what you do with them that counts!

Assembling your composition means paying close attention once again to the balance between new, repeated and varied material. You also need to bear in mind the intention of your piece. For example, club dance music is designed to be very repetitive and so may not give you much opportunity to show the range of skills required in a three-minute piece. On the other hand, the structure of a film score is often determined by the action on screen, which can result in a collage of ideas that don't have a *musical* structure beyond the context of the film. In minimalist music, ideas often unfold gradually, in which case the structure is more about the rate at which these ideas change than actual contrast.

It is important not to be too ambitious in a composition of three minutes' duration – simple structures often work best. If you choose something like ternary (ABA) form, remember that the middle section should offer a contrast – but it shouldn't sound like a totally different piece. And when the A section returns, resist the temptation to 'cut and paste' the opening bars – consider how it can be modified to create a convincing conclusion, aiming for a structure such as ABA[1], perhaps adding a short coda as well.

Large-scale structure

Your study of the set works will help you to understand how keys relate to structure, setting up areas of contrast, expectation, tension and release. Remember, too, that other music that you perform or enjoy listening to can offer ideas on how to structure a piece. For example, think about whether the typical features of a popular song (introduction, verse, chorus, bridge and coda, with perhaps the use of a modulation to lift the final repeat of the chorus) might be adapted to form an instrumental composition.

Pay particular attention to the ways in which composers move smoothly from one idea to another, often making connections between them on the way. Notice the techniques used to avoid losing impetus in a piece, such as overlapping the last chord of a cadence with the first note of the next section, or filling a long note or rest at the end of a phrase with some relevant decoration in a different part.

Make sure that the structure of your own work is aurally clear, and draw attention to it in your commentary. A lack of purposefulness in structure, harmonic language or technique cannot be excused by the explanation 'I want it to sound like this'. If the evidence points to random musings without design and control, your work will not score well under technique.

Exercise 18

1. Track the use of the rhythmic motif stated in the first bar of Beethoven's Violin Concerto in D: explain how it is used harmonically and melodically, to give both variety and unity in the movement as a whole.

2. Identify and explain the ways in which contrasting ideas contribute to the musical structure of a piece you are currently playing or singing.

3. Analyse the structure of a popular song of your choice and show how the form used might be adapted for instrumental composition.

4. Invent a short motif that has the potential to be transformed in some of the ways listed in the table on page 55 and then use some of these methods to turn it into a complete theme.

Communication

When your composition reaches an audience, the process of music communication will be complete. A written score enables your work to be performed by others and a recording will provide one possible representation of your work in audio format.

The score

The layout of the score should follow accepted conventions – refer to published scores to check standard practice. Accuracy of pitch and rhythm are essential. If you use notation software check that the correct clefs have been used to avoid unnecessary leger lines, that key signatures and accidentals are correct, that short notes are beamed correctly and that long notes are not confusingly expressed as multiple tied notes. Find out how to set a small but readable stave size for the score in order to minimise page turns and avoid wasting paper. Check that notes on leger lines don't overlap with the staves above or below.

Note that guitar tablature cannot be offered as an alternative to staff notation. Proficiency in the use of staff notation is a requirement at AS level.

Make sure that you add full performance directions, including dynamics, phrasing, articulation, marks of expression and tempo directions. Piano pedalling marks and essential bowing marks on string parts could also be relevant to your score. These markings not only increase the likelihood that performers will play your piece as you want them to, but they will also provide evidence that you have thought about the varied ways you can use the instruments to the full in your composition.

Check that the staves have been labelled with instrument names, and give your piece a meaningful title which accurately reflects your intentions.

Note that it is perfectly acceptable to submit a handwritten score for your final document. Accuracy, legibility and attention to detail are the main issues whichever format you adopt.

Improvisation

If any sections of your composition use improvisation they should at least be notated in outline. Non-notated improvisation by any performer other than the composer is not credited as composition. In a jazz-style context, for example, you should always provide an outline for any improvised material – even if there is some deviation from it in performance.

The recording

There are various options for recording your composition:

➢ A live performance with intended forces – while this takes time to rehearse and record, it can offer the most realistic realisation of your ideas in most styles of music

➢ A multi-tracked performance in which the various parts are recorded separately and then mixed down into a stereo format

➢ A mixture of intended instruments and substitutions for any that are unavailable, such as playing a double-bass part on a synthesiser

➢ A performance on the piano or other keyboard instrument – this means playing from a piano reduction of the score that will usually omit some of the detail

➢ A sequenced version of the composition – this should be fully edited to represent the expressive intentions as effectively as possible

➢ A mixture of sequenced and live parts – even the inclusion of just one live instrument can transform the often mechanical realisation produced by music software.

Don't worry if your live performance contains some mistakes, as this is preferable to a perfect but bland computer recording that does not convey any life or expression.

It makes sense to consider your options right from the earliest planning days of your composition. If you write for fellow students you will be able to try things out as your ideas develop as well as getting valuable advice from the players themselves. You can use other students, teachers and friends to perform your piece if you wish. You do not have to play in your own composition, but you do have to take charge of the rehearsals and recording; after all, this is part of the assessment and so needs to be your own work.

Check your recording on a conventional playback system and keep backup copies of both the recording and the score. You should not submit data files or use other formats which require specialist equipment or programmes. When you hand in your final folio for assessment, you should include your individual recording for your teacher to listen to and assess.

Arrangement of a lead sheet

If you choose to submit an arrangement instead of a composition you must include a copy of the lead sheet containing the melody and harmony indications with your final submission. The assessment will focus on what you have *added* to this given material and the way in which it has been manipulated and creatively presented. Note that much of the information in the preceding sections is as relevant to arranging as it is to composing.

Many arrangers will have specific jazz or band line-ups for the realisation of their ideas but less conventional uses of medium are also possible and acceptable. Issues for consideration include:

Variety of texture: try to avoid an obvious succession of solos and think about how different pairings or groups of instruments might feature. Try to be imaginative in inventing suitable parts for the rhythm section, especially the bass.

> **Melodic additions**: these could include countermelodies, riffs and fills between phrases.

> **Melodic alteration**: such as adapting a theme to a different style or using anticipations and syncopation to energise the theme.

> **Harmonic realisation**: not just voicing the given chords but also varying the harmonies with added notes and substitutions.

> **Structure**: be imaginative in extending standard structures by adding extra material – an introduction, an ending, interesting features in short solos, new sections that complement the style of the given material.

> **Instrumentation**: ensure that you use your chosen instruments in an idiomatic way, exploiting their possibilities to the full.

> **Tempo and key**: consider altering the original and varying the key and/or tempo at some stage in the arrangement.

It is important to supplement your listening by hearing arrangements relevant to your chosen style. The prescribed recording of Gil Evans / Miles Davis *It Ain't Necessarily So* from *Porgy and Bess* (set for exams up to January 2013) demonstrates a highly creative approach to Gershwin's original material. *Summertime* and *Bess, You is My Woman Now* from the same album (details on page 70) are also well worth studying. Treatments of this type, with plenty of inventive and imaginative writing for instruments, will be more successful than bland transcriptions in which there is no attempt to transform the spirit of the music with the individual fingerprint of the arranger.

Further listening suggestions

Cannonball Adderley's Fiddler on the Roof. Capitol Jazz 542309-2. This includes arrangements of eight numbers from the hit Broadway show.

John Coltrane: *My Favorite Things.* Atlantic 1361-2. A legendary reworking of a song from Rodger and Hammerstein's *The Sound of Music.*

The Bad Plus: *These are the Vistas.* Columbia 510666-2. Two tracks are described as deconstructions of enormous hits: *Heart of Glass* and *Smells like Teen Spirit.*

A example of a form you can use for this can be found in Appendix D1 of the specification.

The commentary and the brief

You will need to give details of your composing brief and provide a commentary about your work. This information shows how you tackled your work and, if done well, can help maximise your marks.

The brief is a concise statement of your composing intentions and you will find it very helpful to discuss ideas with your teacher. The statement may need to be adjusted as work on your composition progresses. Being open to the twists and turns of the creative process may mean your definitive brief will only be certain once the work is well under way.

The purpose of the commentary is to provide:

➢ An outline of the *specific pieces* you have listened to and the ways in which they influenced your composing

➢ An explanation of the processes you used to create the work.

Try to be very clear about the way in which listening connects with your composition – you may want to use short notated snippets of music in your description to explain this.

Simply saying something like 'I really liked the sound of the violin (or guitar) in piece X so I decided to write for this instrument' is not very helpful. It is much more informative to say something along the lines of 'I really liked the sound of the violin in the first movement of Bartók's String Quartet No. X, in particular the extended techniques in the use of the bow such as ...' (and then supply the details), or 'The sound of the lead guitar in Satriani's album *Crystal Planet* opened my eyes to a range of timbres and playing techniques ...' (and then give precise details).

> You may find it useful to keep a log of your listening research as you go along, to remind you of all that you discover and its relevance to your work.

When describing your composing process, try to avoid giving a blow-by-blow account of what is clearly self-evident in the score. A simple, analytical explanation of the main ingredients of your work is important, as is an explanation of the decisions you made about structure, repetition, contrast and so on. Concentrate on explaining *what* you did and, more importantly, *why* you did it.

Spend time on the commentary and aim to show that you are familiar with a range of relevant listening that has influenced your work. Remember that the commentary will provide evidence to the examiner that will help them decide the marks you get for Materials.

Finally

Whether you are a composer or arranger, take pride in being the author of something that is your very own. Be sure to recognise the fine line between unacceptable plagiarism and legitimate, acknowledged instruction from others. Give yourself plenty of time to rework your ideas; you may need to produce several versions of an idea before you get it right. Take the advice of performers around you and work with instruments from the very start of the composing process if you can. You have many options and must give yourself time to consider carefully the choices you make as the work progresses. If a live performance is a realistic possibility for you, enjoy the sense of achievement that such an opportunity brings. If you are able to add a live element to a technologically realised portrayal of your work you may find this can also be very satisfying. Allow time for rehearsal, revisions, and unanticipated technical problems. Above all, take responsibility for a written and audio representation of your work that expresses your musical ideas with accuracy, clarity and integrity.

Introduction to historical study in music

Exam overview

The examination for this unit takes the form of a written paper that lasts for two hours (15 minutes preparation time and 1¾ hours writing time). The question paper is accompanied by a separate booklet (called an 'insert') containing scores and a CD of recorded extracts of music. You are allowed to play the recordings as many times as you wish, within the time available, on a personal CD player equipped with headphones. The paper is in three parts:

Section A (30 marks)

Practice questions for Sections A and B of the paper are provided in *OCR AS Music Listening Tests*, 3rd edition, by Veronica Jamset and Huw Ellis-Williams (Rhinegold, 2011). ISBN 978-1-78038-067-4.

You will be asked several short aural questions based on two or three recorded passages from a piece of *instrumental* music. The music will not be taken from your set works – it may well be from a piece that you are unfamiliar with. You choose extracts from *either* the period 1700–1830 *or* from popular music from 1900 to the present day. You are advised not to spend more than 40 minutes on this section.

Section B (40 marks)

There will be two groups of questions:

➤ The first group is based on a recorded extract and score from *one* of the three orchestral set works that you will have studied (**25 marks**)

➤ The second group is based on one of the three jazz recordings that you will have studied (**15 marks**).

You must study both sets of music. The detailed list for each year is shown on page 70. Check this carefully to make sure you study the right works for the year and session (January or June) that you intend to take the examination.

Section C (20 marks)

You will have to write an essay in answer to a question on an aspect of the background to one or more of the six set works that you have studied. There will be three questions for you to choose from. Although you only have to answer one question, some of the questions are likely to require writing about more than one of the works.

You are allowed 15 minutes at the start of the examination to read through the paper, look at the scores for Sections A and B, find the tracks on the CD and get yourself organised. Most importantly, this gives you a chance to *listen to all your extracts* – make the most of this opportunity.

Content

The study of any sort of history involves gathering evidence, establishing facts and interpreting them. Music history is no different: it depends on analysing evidence.

Evidence

Evidence includes contemporary documents (that is, documents from the day) such as newspaper advertisements, reports and reviews, letters, such as those to or from the composer or others involved in a first performance, bills, records of fees paid to performers or instrument makers, and the diaries and journals of informed commentators of the time. Other types of evidence may be less reliable. For instance, biographies – even when written soon after the composer's lifetime – may include misremembered facts or the biographer may have let his own views influence the account.

The primary document, if it still exists, is often the composer's autograph score or an original recording of a jazz work – although composers sometimes revise their works for later performances and jazz musicians frequently devise new versions of previously recorded tracks. Sometimes an early published edition in which the composer has made corrections or other annotations (such as suggestions to a pupil for fingering or realising ornaments) may provide evidence. Further clues to how 18th-century music was performed may come from 'teach yourself' books that were published at the time – these were often weighty treatises that explain in detail the performing conventions of the day. The 18th-century composer, Quantz, wrote one on playing the flute, and Mozart's father, Leopold, wrote about playing the violin.

> An 'autograph score' is one in the composer's own handwriting.

Facts

A straight chronology of events, or list of dates when music was composed or first performed is one type of starting-point. Another might be geography – where were things happening? Whether a composer was Austrian or Italian, or whether a jazz band was playing in New Orleans or New York, might have made a difference to the style of the music. Who taught whom? Which performers are known to have worked together? Piecing together the trail that leads from one musician to another can cast light on our understanding of their music.

> When writing about dates, be careful not to confuse years with centuries. We live in the 21st century, but the years begin with 20, not 21. Similarly, 1780 is not in the 17th century but in the 18th century.

Interpretation

The evidence is analysed, hypotheses are explored, and judgements are made. The purpose is to help us understand why the music is as it is, how the composer would have expected it to sound and what it is 'about'. To answer these questions we need to apply different sorts of analytical skill.

In the examination you will be expected to be able to discuss what is known about the background context of the set works (particularly in Section C). You are not expected to do your own historical research but doing some additional reading will help you form a better picture in your mind. Some useful sources are listed in this guide.

You are expected to have studied the music itself very closely, first-hand, and to be able to discuss it using technical language. To do this successfully you will need to develop specialised analytic skills. These are discussed at the end of this section.

Reception

'Reception' is a word used to describe how a work was regarded by audiences, critics and performers of the day as well as how perceptions of a work have changed over time. For instance, in the 19th century some writers referred to Mozart as 'divine' because his gifts were thought to be so great. Twentieth-century writers have looked more closely at the human being, the man behind the music, and found a much less 'divine' personality. This has not meant that his music has been valued less, but it does mean that our perception of what we hear and how we make sense of it may be different in the 21st century.

How the first performance of a piece of music is received depends on what the audience are expecting. If they are familiar with the style they may appreciate the work's inventiveness. Eighteenth-century audiences were used to hearing much new music, often specially composed for the occasion. If a work didn't sound up-to-the-minute they might complain that it seemed old-fashioned and stale, although if it was very innovative they could be shocked.

Study of the history of music in the mid-18th century was confined to a few enthusiasts. Awareness and appreciation of old music began to develop among musicians towards the end of the century and to spread more widely during the 19th century. By the 20th century it was common for orchestral concert programmes to give pride of place to the music of earlier composers, especially those who were by then recognised as great masters, while performances of new music became less common.

Conversely, jazz and popular music still depend on a constant stream of new music, although they too have their histories and there is a keen appreciation of landmark performances of the past.

Transmission

How does music become known to an audience beyond those present at a first performance? Today, communications are immediate. Until the advent of photocopiers and computers with music-notation software, parts had to be copied by hand. Copying played an important role, too, in how students, composers and connoisseurs got to know new music. This was a slow process. But, by the end of the 18th century, the demand for music to perform at home had fuelled rapid growth in music publishing and composers in the next century were increasingly able to earn part of their living from sales of their music. But there was no copyright protection, so pirated editions and handwritten copies would quickly circulate if a first performance had been a success.

Connoisseurs (people with an expert understanding of an art) have been as important in music as in any other art form. For instance, many aristocrats were accomplished performers on instruments and some composed as well. They often had enough interest and wealth to commission new music, employ musicians and to accumulate libraries of music to perform and study.

Composers frequently dedicated music to them. Sponsorship is still important, although today funds are more likely to be channelled through charitable trusts, broadcasting companies and government agencies such as Arts Council England.

In the late 19th century, greater prosperity enabled more people to purchase pianos and sheet music to play at home, both coming down in price as a result of industrial manufacturing processes. This was followed, in the early 20th century, by radio and recording, which widened the audience for music further still. No longer was it necessary to journey to a large city to hear celebrated performers, or to pay high box-office prices – everyone could access the latest music cheaply and immediately. Recordings by different artists (or the same ones on different occasions) could easily be compared. Popular audiences became increasingly knowledgeable about the music they liked.

Reception and transmission are aspects of the study of the history of music that you may be asked about in Section C.

Some people find the term 'analysis' rather off-putting, but it simply means discovering how music works – an essential skill for any musician. It helps us to understand how styles and genres change over time, to trace the influence of one sort of music on another, to explain what appears to be a radical innovation – perhaps dispelling myths that portray it as one man's revolution overnight – and to categorise trends and identify common characteristics.

You will need to develop some analytic skills for the listening paper. In Section A you will be applying these to understanding an extract of *unfamiliar music*, listening and answering questions 'on the hoof'. In Section B you will already know the music well and will be expected, therefore, to be able to answer more probing analytic questions.

What is involved in analysis? First, you need a keen ear – you must be able to distinguish one instrument from another, one part from another, the treble, the bass, the keys, chords, cadences, repetition and variation, structure, and so on. Secondly, you need knowledge – to be able to identify specific techniques used in the music, such as sequences, pizzicato, imitation or pedal notes, and to give them their technical names. Finally, you need to be able to describe and explain how the music works in your own words.

Writing about music needs practice. There are many short exercises in this guide designed to help you build up the skills you need in order to be able to answer confidently in an examination. Work through them all slowly and don't skip any. Then you will be ready to get the greatest possible benefit from working through complete practice tests.

Analytic techniques

Section A

This section of your exam is not just a test of aural perception: you will need to understand musical notation, know technical terms and be confident about identifying keys, chords and cadences. The recordings are accompanied by a skeleton score and you may be asked to write in a missing phrase of melody, notate part of a bass line, name chords or identify ornaments.

Whichever extract you choose (1A on instrumental music from the period 1700–1830 or 1B on instrumental popular music from 1900 to the present day) it will usually consist of two or at most three short passages separated by short breaks. These will be labelled 'passage 1i', 'passage 1ii' and 'passage 1iii', and will all be from different sections of a single piece of music. Sometimes the second and third passages will be actual variations of a theme that was given in the first passage but, more often, they will simply use some of the same material as the first passage but in slightly different ways. As well as questions related to tonality and the expressive use of instrumental techniques, you might also be asked about the ways in which the later passages vary material from the first one.

A skeleton score gives an outline of the music, often on two staves, with enough detail for you to follow it as you listen, but it also has quite a lot of information missing. Bar numbers and CD timings are printed in the score to help you follow the recording.

Whichever extract you choose, its musical language will be tonal. The questions are a test of whether you can really hear the techniques you have been learning and using in your exercises for Section A of the composing unit.

Tonality The scores will be straightforward, so that the notes are not too dense on the page or cluttered with too many other symbols. The examiners are more interested in what you can hear and whether you understand the tonal style than in setting you complicated writing tasks. But you do need to be able to read treble and bass clefs confidently, and to be able to notate pitches and common rhythmic patterns accurately, because you will be asked to notate short passages (on the score) in both clefs. Most importantly, you must be sure of your keys, not just recognising them from key signatures at the beginning of the score but hearing and identifying modulations that happen in the course of the extract. Making sure you can do this should be an important part of your preparation.

Ornamentation Other aspects of the music that you might be asked to identify or explain include variation techniques, inessential notes and ornamentation. The sign for an ornament might be omitted and you could be asked to write it in the correct position on the score, or to give its name and describe what it does. Three of the most common types of ornament are played by the solo violin in the first movement of Beethoven's Concerto in D:

➢ A **trill** (*tr*) consists of a rapid alternation between the printed note and the note above. The soloist plays an exceptionally long series of trills in bars 205–216. (There are many shorter examples in the first movement of the Vivaldi Bassoon Concerto, for example bars 29–31.)

➢ A **turn** (∾) starts on the note above the printed note, followed by the printed note itself, then the note below it, and finally the printed note once more. In bar 342 the soloist plays three turns, which decorate a rising scale.

➢ In the first four bars of the solo part (bars 89–92) Beethoven adds **grace notes**. Although notated as very small semiquavers, they have no precise rhythmic value but are to be played immediately before the beat, stealing a little value from the previous note.

➢ An **acciaccatura** (pronounced *at-chak-ka-toora*) is a note printed in small type with a slash through its tail (♪). It is also played as quickly as possible, usually just before the beat, according to the context. There are examples in the solo bassoon part in Vivaldi's concerto, bar 35.

➢ An **appoggiatura**, however, is played on the beat, leaning onto the main note.

More on the appoggiatura There are clear examples of appoggiaturas in the opening of the first movement of Vivaldi's Bassoon Concerto, in the 2nd violin part:

In different recordings of this piece, you may find that the appoggiatura varies in interpretation, giving contrasting amounts of weight and duration to how it is played. The appoggiatura can take up to half the value of the main note, but with slightly more weight on the first note. In contrast, it could be much shorter (and lighter), more like the phrase in bar 2 ('short-long, short-long'). There is no fixed rule on what portion of the principal note the appoggiatura should take.

A valid question about the notation of bars 1 and 2 is to consider: 'What is the difference between bars 1 and 2? In the performance on my recording they sound very similar. Why are they notated differently in the score?' The answer lies in the harmonic function of the first note of each pair: a true appoggiatura forms a dissonance, drawing attention to it because of its position on the stronger part of the beat; spice is given to the music by the need to resolve this dissonance. The two appoggiaturas in bar 1 create this effect: the A and F♯ are both dissonant against chord I of E minor. However, in bar 2 the demisemiquavers A, F♯, D♯ and B fit over the B major chord (V), and the G and E demisemiquavers that follow fit against the subsequent chord I of E minor. Therefore, in bar 2 the first note of each pair is the harmony note and the longer dotted semiquavers are actually almost accented passing-notes, which form a dissonance against the underlying harmony in that bar.

> This type of dotted rhythm, where a short note value is followed by a longer one, is known as a Lombardic rhythm or Scotch Snap.

Instruments and textures

Throughout the AS course, techniques for combining instruments will keep coming under the spotlight and you should expect one or two questions about this aspect of the music in these extracts. As well as identifying instruments you should be prepared to recognise common performing techniques like glissando, pizzicato and the use of a mute.

If you are asked to *describe* the texture of a passage it is important to give as much detail as you can: explain if parts are in unison or doubled an octave above or below, identify the instruments and explain exactly who is doing what. If the texture is imitative, be specific – say which instrument begins, which comes in next, what the pitch interval between these two entries is, and so on.

Variation techniques

Whether the passages in the extract you have chosen are described as variations or not, they will certainly be closely related to one another. You will be asked to identify the techniques that have been used to vary the original theme. This might be through change of key, tempo or harmony, different melodic decoration or changes in instrumentation and texture.

> For discussion and examples of variation techniques see *OCR AS Music Listening Tests, 3rd edition* (Rhinegold Education, 2011).

The use of variation techniques is not confined to the 18th century – if you choose extract 1B you will find that similar questions are asked. Almost all music includes variation of previously heard material and the techniques used are still important to composers today – could this include you, in your work for Section B of the composing unit? And, of course, variation is one of the most significant ingredients in jazz improvisation.

If you decide to answer questions on the popular music extract (1B) remember that it could come from before or after the period of the set jazz recordings that you will be studying (which come from the years 1920–1960). The style of the music may or may not be influenced by jazz. However, the types of question will be similar to those for extract 1A. There may be clear use of variation techniques but the extract may be from film music in which the original theme is altered significantly or reduced to one or two motifs for dramatic reasons.

Exercise 19

The following extract is a skeleton score of bars 43 to 63 in Beethoven's Violin Concerto in D, first movement. Listen to a recording of this extract while following this skeleton score:

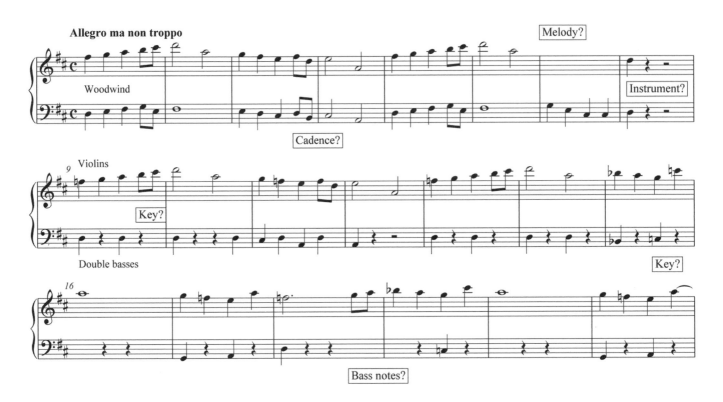

1. What sort of cadence is heard at bars 3^4–4^1?

2. **On the score** complete the melody in bar 7.

3. New instruments enter in bar 8: name **one** of them and describe the rhythm it plays.

4 a. Identify the key of the music in bars 9–12.

   b. Identify the key of the music in bars 15^3–16.

5. **On the score** write in the missing bass notes on beats 18^4 and 19^1.

6. Briefly describe the music played by the violas and cellos in bars 9–21.

7. Comment on the phrase structure of the extract.

When you have answered all these questions check your answers against your own copy of the study score. Compare your answers with ours on page 69.

Section B

There will be three tracks on your CD for this section of the paper. The first two of these will contain *different performances* of an extract from one of the three set orchestral works. They will be labelled 'Extract 2A' and 'Extract 2B' on the question paper. You may not bring copies of the scores into the examination room but you will be given a full score of the extract in the insert booklet (note that this score will not include CD timings).

The first few questions are usually about the **notation** of the score, such as the meaning of abbreviations or signs. You could be asked to transpose a clarinet or trumpet part into sounding pitch, or to write out on a treble or bass stave a viola phrase that is printed in the C clef. These are questions that you need to practise during the course – don't leave these skills until the night before the exam, especially since they are also likely to be needed when answering other types of questions.

There may well be one or two questions about **tonality** and tonal devices in this extract – a chord, a cadence, modulations and key relationships, sequences and pedal notes can all crop up. Recognising these in an orchestral score also needs practice.

You may be asked to describe the **texture** of the extract, to compare the passage with an earlier or later statement of the same theme (for which you will have to rely on your memory!), or to comment on how typical it is of this composer. Keep 'compare' questions in your mind as you study each score: notice when the woodwind are silent and when they play, whether they double the strings or have independent parts, what the difference is between the brass contributing a melody and simply filling out a chord, or which instruments sustain a dominant pedal.

You will be expected to be able to place the extract within the movement as a whole. To do this, you must know the outline **structure** of the movement and be able to recognise typical features of each section within it. You might be asked, for instance, whether an extract containing the second subject is from the exposition or the recapitulation (the clue usually lies in the key). Or, you might be asked to describe significant features of the music that comes before or after the actual extract.

The two recordings of the extract will have been chosen because they contrast in sound. Their interpretation of features such as tempo, dynamics, phrasing and articulation may differ. The orchestras themselves may not be made up the same way. One of the excerpts might have been recorded by a large orchestra of modern instruments while the other was recorded by a much smaller ensemble of 'period' instruments, with relatively few string players to each part. The latter type of performance might also be at a lower pitch than its modern equivalent, reflecting the fact that pitch in the period 1700–1830 was slightly lower than is usual today.

Research into how music was performed in the past has also made it possible to use performing techniques that produce sounds more like the ones that the original composers would have expected to

Extract 2

'Period' instruments are usually modern reconstructions that allow the performer to recreate the type of sound that might have been heard when early music was first performed.

hear. This approach to performing music of the past is often referred to as **authentic** because it is said to be more faithful to the composer's intentions. Another view is that the music will sound different on modern instruments, but not necessarily worse, and that the composers of the past might well have welcomed the different sound.

You will not be asked to make a judgement about which of the performances is 'better', but you do need to understand some of the issues that will have influenced the two conductors in reaching their interpretative decisions.

Try to hear more than one type of recorded performance of each of your orchestral set works: all of them have been recorded many times during the last 50 years and historical research into styles of playing has influenced many of the more recent conductors.

Study the section on 'The score' in the next chapter (page 71) and work through all the exercises in it. This will give you the information and basic techniques needed to get started. Then tackle one of the three orchestral set works. Listen with the score to more than one recording if at all possible. The more often you do this, the more easily you will be able to make musical sense of the score for yourself. Then, when the *sound* of each piece has begun to take root inside your head, study the relevant section in the chapter on the orchestral set works. Use your reading to inform your hearing – not the other way round. Don't treat the recordings as 'add-ons' to the information you read.

Extract 3   The third extract will be from one of the three set jazz recordings (see the list on page 70). There will be no score, so the questions will usually be about things that you can hear clearly on the recording.

There will be questions about the instruments and how they are used. You may be asked to describe the texture of a particular passage. Your answer should show that you understand the role of each instrument, whether frontline or rhythm section, and you should be prepared to describe particular features of the music that each plays, including any special effects such as glissando or the use of a mute. You should also be able to recognise compositional devices used in the music, such as call-and-response, secondary rag or collective improvisation.

You may be asked to relate the extract to an earlier part of the piece that is not heard on the recording. You will need to remember the outline structure of the whole work and know it well enough to recognise exactly where the recorded extract comes in it. You will be expected to be able to describe the music that follows the extract, so you will need to be sure of the order of solo and chorus sections and be able to describe their main features.

You should know the names of the main performers in the band, particularly those who make a significant contribution to the music, including soloists and the rhythm section.

Section C

The last question in the examination will be an essay on one or more of the set works. Further details and practice questions are given in the Section C questions chapter of this book, starting on page 151.

Answers for Exercise 19

1. Imperfect (it comes to rest on chord V).

2. Check against the first oboe part in the study score.

3. Any of horns, trumpets, timpani. Rhythm is crotchets.

4   a. D minor

    b. F major

5. Check against the double-bass part.

6. 'Constant triplets' is the short answer, but you might want to add any of: an octave apart; quietly; mainly by step but with some broken-chord leaps; or add a word that describes how you hear the effect, such as 'swirling' or 'busy'.

7. At first, balanced four-bar phrases; an eight-bar melody consisting of 4+4; repeated with modulations in bars 9–16; but with an extra two-bar sequence to modulate back to the tonic minor; then those last four bars repeated; the last note held, stopping the even flow.

Set works

For Sections B and C of the paper you have to study six set works (described by OCR as the 'prescribed repertoire') – three orchestral scores from the 18th and early 19th centuries, plus three jazz recordings, from the period 1920–1960.

It is very important to check carefully that you are studying the right combination of pieces for the year and session in which you are going to take the exam:

Orchestral scores

June 2012 to January 2014	1. Vivaldi: Concerto in E minor for Bassoon and Orchestra, RV484 (first movement) 2. Haydn: *Drum Roll* Symphony No.103 in E♭, Hob.I:103 (fourth movement) 3. Beethoven: Concerto in D for Violin and Orchestra, Op. 61, (first movement)
June 2014 to January 2016	1. Handel: *Water Music* Suite No.2 in D, HWV349 (Allegro, Alla Hornpipe, Menuet, Lentement and Bourrée) 2. Mozart: Concerto No. 4 in E♭ for Horn and Orchestra, K.495 (third movement) 3. Beethoven: Symphony No. 5 in C minor, Op. 67 (first movement)

Jazz recordings

June 2011 to January 2013	1. Louis Armstrong and His Hot Five: *Alligator Crawl* (1927) from *Louis Armstrong 25 Greatest Hot Fives and Hot Sevens*, Living Era AJA 5171 (ASIN B000001H15) 2. Charlie Parker: *Ko-Ko* (1945), from *Ornithology: Classic Recordings 1945–1947*, Naxos Jazz Legends 8.120571 (ASIN B00005US4G) 3. Gil Evans/Miles Davis: *It Ain't Necessarily So* from *Porgy and Bess* (1958), Sony Jazz CK65141 (ASIN B000024F6M)
June 2013 to January 2015	1. Louis Armstrong and His Hot Five: *Hotter Than That* (1927) from *Louis Armstrong 25 Greatest Hot Fives & Hot Sevens*, Living Era AJA 5171 (ASIN B000001H15) 2. Duke Ellington: *Koko* (1940) from *Cotton Tail: Classic Recordings, Vol. 7* (1940), Naxos Jazz Legends 8.120738 (ASIN B00030B9AC) 3. Miles Davis: *Boplicity* from *Birth of the Cool* (1949), on *Birth of the Cool, Rudy Van Gelder (RVG) Edition* (original recording remastered), Capitol Jazz/Blue Note Records 7 24353 0117 2 7 (ASIN B00005614M). [The original recording can also be found on the CD specified for use with the previous OCR Music specification: Capitol Jazz 0777 7 92862 2 5 (ASIN B000005HF9).]

Note that any edition and any recording of the orchestral scores may be used but you *must* make sure that the jazz recordings you study are *exactly* the ones listed above.

Orchestral scores

You will be provided with a copy of the music for Extract 2 in the examination paper. The extract will be from one of your three prescribed orchestral scores.

It won't look exactly the same as the copy that you have been using during your course but it will use the standard conventions and format found in most modern editions. Bars will be numbered from the beginning of the extract, so are unlikely to coincide with the bar numbering of the complete piece. To be able to answer the questions about the work sucessfully you will need to understand some of the conventions for notating and interpreting scores.

> Bars are usually numbered from the first complete bar onwards and superscript numerals are used for beats, so bar 8^1 means the first beat of bar 8.

The score

Editions

Most scores you use in class will probably be miniature, pocket or study editions. Modern conductors use much larger full scores that allow them to read the notes more easily while standing. Scores of orchestral music were rarely published in printed form before the 19th century. In the early and mid-18th century, performances were usually directed from the harpsichord, often by the composer himself. If the composer was also the soloist in a concerto the solo part could be incomplete, the remainder being improvised on the night. The performance was often a very last-minute affair – it is no exaggeration to say that the ink on the page was sometimes still wet! The score was the master document from which a copyist rushed to prepare individual parts for the performers.

During the 19th century a public market for printed scores developed, sometimes copied and published without the composer's permission. The reputation of a work could spread widely, far beyond the big cities where there were opportunities to hear it performed, and people began to want to get to know fashionable pieces, not just hear them once only. Sometimes the first opportunity to hear a work would be in an arrangement for piano given by a touring virtuoso. Playing piano-duet versions of symphonies and overtures at home was a popular way of getting to know the classics of the orchestral repertoire in the late 19th and early 20th centuries.

With the advent of recording and broadcasting, and the growth of international tours, opportunities to hear and rehear orchestral music in different interpretations increased, and with these came a demand for cheaply-printed, pocket-sized scores for study purposes. Audiences began to be knowledgeable and critical about how music was performed. They could compare different approaches of conductors and performers, who often consciously tried to impose their own personal stamp on the music.

In the second half of the 20th century performers and scholars everywhere became concerned to ensure that the scores used in the preparation of performances reproduced what the composer had originally written more reliably – in other words, that they were authentic. Editors sought out manuscripts and the earliest printed editions, comparing them and trying to resolve problems or discrepancies between them in the light of what they knew about the conventions of the composer's time – in other words, performance practice. The result of such careful scholarship is often the publication of what is called an Urtext (original text) edition, which usually includes a detailed account of how the different sources have been used. Critical scores have also become common; these give a great deal more background information about the genesis of the music, and if the composer left any rough drafts of the work these might be included as well.

OCR does not require you to use any particular edition or recording of the orchestral scores. Depending on what your school or college has in its collection you may be working from a recent Urtext or from a much earlier, edited score. You should be aware that there might be differences, and some of the detail in the extract used in the exam might not be identical to the score you have been using. However, it is not necessary to study more than one edition of any of the orchestral set works.

Notation

Most modern scores use a standard format that may be different from the original layout used by the composer. Instruments are grouped into sections – woodwind at the top, followed by horns, then any other brass and percussion, then strings at the bottom. Music for woodwind and string instruments is printed in order of pitch – highest at the top, lowest at the bottom. If there is a solo instrument (as in your Vivaldi and Beethoven concertos), its part is usually shown immediately above the strings.

In your Vivaldi score there may be two further staves at the bottom, labelled *cembalo* or *continuo*. The bass line will usually be the same as the cello part, but any chords in the treble (probably in small print to show that the editor has supplied them) will be a suggested realisation of what an early 18th-century keyboard (harpsichord or organ) or lute player might have improvised.

Instrument names are often in Italian, but most are easily recognisable (such as *flauto*, a flute). Oboes and bassoons (*fagotti*) were the original staples of the woodwind section, with the flute making an occasional appearance. Clarinets were added towards the end of the 18th century. By about 1800 the woodwind were usually scored in pairs (two flutes, two oboes, two clarinets and two bassoons) – a layout known as **double woodwind**. However, Beethoven only uses one flute in his Violin Concerto in D.

Horns (*corni*) were also usually used in pairs in the 18th century and are always placed above the trumpets in the score, reflecting the fact that they are often used to blend with the woodwind. In some scores trumpets (*trombe*) may be named as *clarino* – be careful not to confuse these with clarinets.

Throughout the 18th century, the percussion normally consisted of just a pair of timpani played by one person. The notes to which they are to be tuned are given at the beginning of the score and are usually the tonic and dominant of the main key (D and A in the Beethoven; E♭ and B♭ in the Haydn).

Double basses (*contrabassi*) usually play the same notes as the cellos, but sound an octave lower.

Occasionally a composer specifies cellos alone, usually to provide a slightly lighter texture: for example, in bars 166–170 in the first movement of Beethoven's Violin Concerto in D (but notice how the double basses come back in bars 170–171, playing on the strong beats against the rest of the strings). To get a fuller texture, the composer may also divide a string part between the available players: for example, later in the same movement at bar 280, Beethoven has written repeated semiquaver 3rds for the violas. Although many chords can be played on string instruments (known as 'double-stopping'), such as the C major chord for first violins in bar 280 (which can be played by moving the bow quickly across all four strings), the violas must divide their two notes (C and E below middle C). This is because the C is the viola's lowest string and it is impossible to play two notes at the same time on a single string.

If a pair of wind instruments has only a single line of music then both are expected to play – unless it is marked *solo* to show that only the first instrument is required. The direction *a 2* will appear if they are then to resume playing in unison. The figures 1. and 2., or the use of upward or downward stems on the notes, may also indicate which instrument is to play.

Scores did not specify how many string players were required – it depended on factors such as the number of wind parts, size of the venue, what could be afforded and availability of players. The author of the *Musikalisches Lexicon* (musical dictionary), published in 1802, recommended six first violins, six second violins, four violas, four cellos and three double basses for symphonies – 23 string players in total – although both smaller and larger string sections than this were used during the 18th century, depending on circumstances. The orchestra that played for Haydn in London in the 1790s comprised around 60 players. In comparison, a modern symphony orchestra is likely to have around 60 string players.

You need to develop an ability to 'hear' internally the sounds that the score suggests – not just the melodic lines, but the rhythms and harmonies, the timbres of individual instruments, and the effects of combining them in different types of texture. This will become easier after studying and repeatedly listening to the music.

As well as treble and bass clefs you will need to learn to find your way around the C clef (𝄡). This is used for several mid-range instruments which would otherwise need a lot of leger lines if notated using either treble or bass clefs.

Wherever the C clef is placed on a stave, the stave-line through its centre fixes the position of middle C, as shown right. The alto C clef straddles the middle line of the stave and is used for viola parts,

Clefs

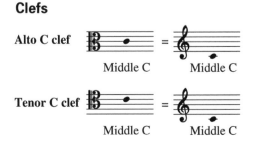

while the tenor C clef is one line higher and is used for notes in the upper registers of the bassoon, trombone and cello. The two examples below are from Haydn's Symphony No. 103 in E♭ (fourth movement). Compare how using the tenor clef in the first example reduces the number of leger lines, in contrast to the second example which uses the bass clef only.

Exercise 20

If you are asked to rewrite a C-clef passage into either the treble or bass clef, use middle C as a reference point and check every few notes that you haven't slipped in pitch as you go. When you are asked to write out a part in a different clef always remember to put the correct key signature at the beginning of the stave.

1. Write out the following viola part on a sheet of manuscript paper, using the treble clef. In this example the F♯ in the key signature lies unusually low on the stave.

2. Write out the following bassoon part twice: (i) using the bass clef and (ii) using the treble clef:

If you look at the lists of instruments at the beginning of your Haydn and Beethoven scores you will almost certainly see the letters E♭ (Haydn) and D (Beethoven) beside the names of the horns (*corni*), and notice that these parts have no key signatures. In the 18th and early 19th centuries, the number and range of notes that a single instrument could play was very limited – horns (and trumpets) usually had to be pitched in the tonic key of the piece. The composer always wrote the part as though it was in C major: this was an indication to the player of where the notes lay on the instrument, not of their actual pitch. For example, at the beginning of the last movement of Symphony No. 103, Haydn's horn players read:

However, the instruments actually sound (i.e. at concert pitch) as follows:

Therefore, horns sound a major 6th lower than the notes written for them, and trumpets in E♭ sound a minor 3rd higher.

In Beethoven's Violin Concerto in D, horns in D sound a minor 7th lower than the notes written for them:

However, trumpets in D sound a tone higher. Look at your score and listen to the trumpet parts in the first movement of Beethoven's Violin Concerto in D. From bar 346 onwards, the octaves are written as G but you can hear clearly that they are repeating the dominant note A very quietly in the background (with the timpani).

Modern horns (almost always pitched in F) and trumpets (most often in B♭) are still notated as though they were in C major, but the addition of valves has made them more versatile. Performers can now modulate freely and play chromatic notes.

Clarinets are also notated as transposing instruments. Their pitch is most often either B♭ or A, depending on which suits the key of the piece better. If you look at the openings of your Haydn and Beethoven scores you will see that, confusingly, clarinets in both pieces have key signatures of one flat (F major). This is because the B♭ clarinet (in the Haydn movement) sounds a tone lower than is written – therefore, its key signature has to be a tone higher than the key of the piece (which is E♭ major). The A clarinet (in the Beethoven) sounds a minor 3rd

> When the score shows the note C for a transposing instrument, the sound (concert pitch) that the instrument will produce will be the note given beside its name in the list at the beginning of the score.

lower so its written key signature must be a minor 3rd higher than the key of the piece (which is D major):

Learning to identify quickly what the concert-pitch notes are that horns, trumpets and clarinets are playing is a skill which you must practise. You will almost certainly be given a few bars of music for one of these transposing instruments in the examination question paper and be asked to write them out at concert pitch. If you can become confident at doing this then you will also find it easier to identify chords and keys accurately in your scores.

Exercise 21

1. Write out at concert pitch the following bars for clarinet. (Remember to put the appropriate key signature.)

2. Look in your score of the first movement of Beethoven's Violin Concerto in D at bars 269–272:

    a. Without looking at the string parts, work out the key of the music and name the chords played by woodwind and brass.

    b. What position in the chord is the note played by:

        (i) the timpani in bar 269

        (ii) the horn in bar 270?

    c. Listen to this extract carefully, following the woodwind, brass and timpani parts.

Interpretation

Getting the notes right is the first priority for an orchestra but there's more to a good performance than just that. How the notes are played is important. Most composers will have given some guidance about this in their scores using performance directions. These musical terms are often written in Italian – you will need to learn the meanings of the words and symbols covered in the following sections.

Allegro – the word used by all three composers at the start of your orchestral scores. Originally, it suggested that the music should be performed in a 'lively' way, but it gradually came to be understood as indicating a fast tempo. In the first movement of his Violin Concerto in D Beethoven limits the notion of speed by adding *ma non troppo* ('but not too much'). In your Haydn score the composer adds *con spirito* ('with spirit'), which is usually interpreted as emphasising the lively character of the music. Haydn also has a different time signature: $\frac{2}{2}$ or ¢ (*alla breve* or 'cut time'), which means that the beats are minims, not crotchets as in Beethoven's $\frac{4}{4}$ or C ('common time'). The simple duple time signature helps the music to feel more lively.

Tempo

Exercise 22

Listen to the opening eight bars of each of your three set works. Compare the speed (tempo) of the crotchets (remember the Vivaldi is moving mainly in quavers). Which work sounds the slowest? If you have a metronome to hand, check your answer.

It is rare to hear a performance of any long movement from the 18th or early 19th century in which the tempo is exactly the same all the way through. Particularly in concertos, there will be moments when the soloist may want to use **rubato**, which allows freedom to be more expressive by varying the tempo. Furthermore, conductors vary considerably in the way they bring movements to an end: some slow down a little; some a great deal; some hardly at all. Practise identifying fluctuations in tempo when you listen to different interpretations of your set works so that you can be quick to spot the use of rubato in the recordings you are given to compare in the examination.

There are many different (articulation) signs that composers use to tell performers how to play each note: whether to detach it (*staccato*), accent it (*marcato*), hold it firmly (*tenuto*), or run it smoothly into the next note (*legato*). How performers understand these signs changes over time, and their meaning might vary slightly from composer to composer. When you compare recordings of your orchestral set works you may notice that one conductor consistently interprets staccato markings as a very slight shortening of notes, while another might cut them much shorter. Get into the habit of listening out for these very subtle differences in interpretation.

Articulation

Some articulation signs mean specific things to different instrumentalists: for example, the way slurs are used in a melody tells wind players how to tongue it; for string players it suggests how the melody should be bowed. There are some other signs that apply only to string instruments:

➢ **Pizzicato** (usually abbreviated to 'pizz.') tells players when to pluck the strings

➢ **Arco** tells them when to resume using the bow

➢ **Tremolo** is notated by strokes through the beam of the note to indicate rapid repetitions: the number of strokes determines

the speed of the repetitions (tremolo technique also applies to timpani parts).

The two strokes through the crotchet and minims in the music example to the left indicate that performers are to repeat the note to its full value using semiquavers. It may also be used in this way for timpani parts, but a long roll is often written as *tr* (trill).

Dynamics   In the Baroque period composers wrote very few dynamic markings into their scores, as they expected performers to be thoroughly familiar with the conventions of the day. In a solo concerto the orchestral *tutti* (sections where all parts play the *ritornello*) would sound as loud whether they were marked *f* (*forte*) or not. The solo episodes were usually more lightly scored, however the orchestral parts might have indications for *p* (*piano*); alternatively, fewer instruments might be used in these accompanying passages. Vivaldi also marks as *p* the many unison descending scale passages that occur in the first movement of his Bassoon Concerto in E minor, to create a contrast in dynamics. Haydn is quite sparing in his dynamic markings in the last movement of his Symphony No 103. Many of the more lightly-scored passages are marked *p*, but notice that he distinguishes between the markings *f* and *ff* (*fortissimo*) – the latter is used several times for the more dramatic moments. Haydn does not use hairpin signs ⟨ ══ ⟩ or the words *crescendo* and *diminuendo*.

Exercise 23

1. Listen to your recording of the passage in bars 217–263 in your Haydn score. It starts *p*, is marked *f* at bar 247, then *ff* at bar 258. Does the conductor on your recording make abrupt changes to the dynamic level at these points, or is there a long, smooth crescendo throughout this extract?

2. Listen to your recording of bars 18–31 in your Beethoven score.

    ➢ You will notice that Beethoven was very precise about dynamic markings and fond of extreme contrasts. In bar 22 the clarinets and bassoons make a small *crescendo* but the strings continue playing softly. The *diminuendo* in bar 25 brings the music back to an even quieter level (*pp*) before the dramatic surprise of bar 28.

    ➢ The outburst in bar 28 is a surprise not only because of the sheer volume of sound (tutti *ff*), but also because the chord is unexpected. It is an interrupted cadence, but instead of the more usual chord of B minor (chord vi in D major) Beethoven uses a chord of B♭ major (chord vi in D minor). Nothing in the previous 27 bars has prepared our ears for this shift.

    ➢ Beethoven is also fond of *fz* and *sf* (*sforzando*) for single notes, making them stab and die away (for example, woodwind in bar 7). Notice, too, that he always marks the theme throughout the movement as *dolce* ('sweetly').

Although there are machines that can measure noise levels accurately in decibels, judging the changes in dynamic levels throughout a piece of music is very subjective. When you listen to your set works try to notice how different conductors handle dynamics: perhaps one interpretation will seem to work better than another? Ask yourself whether the contrasts are too sudden, too extreme, and whether there is enough contrast, or too much?

Orchestral scores contain a great deal of information and to begin following scores you may want to concentrate on keeping up with the music, probably by following the melody, whichever part it is in. As you become more familiar with the sound, and how it relates to the layout, practise trying to hear how different instruments perform different roles in the texture. For example, can you hear:

➢ When the flute doubles the first violins an octave above, for instance in your Beethoven score, bars 28–29?

➢ When the bassoon plays a pedal in the middle of the texture, for instance in your Haydn score, bars 82–89?

➢ Which instrument supplies the 3rd of the chord in your Vivaldi score, bar 7^1?

Get into the habit of noticing the effect of different timbres, how various combinations of instruments are used, and how a composer can create a crescendo by piling on the instruments rather than just increasing the dynamic levels.

As you listen, sometimes focus on details, sometimes listen to the whole: your eye on the score can identify techniques and effects which your ear may only be dimly aware of at first.

From time to time you may notice something that strikes you as an effective technique or combination of instruments that might be adapted for use in your own compositions. You could begin by experimenting with the variety of expressive sounds that can be obtained by different sorts of doubling.

Vivaldi: Bassoon Concerto in E minor, RV 484

Antonio Vivaldi (1678–1741) was for most of his working life employed by the Pio Ospedale della Pietà in Venice. He was appointed 'maestro di violino', a post renewed every year (there were a few years when the governors of the Pietà did not renew his appointment). He took holy orders in the church – he was famously known as 'the Red Priest' because of his red hair. As his reputation grew he spent less time in the Pietà itself. He had a busy life as a violinist, composer and a director of operas, travelling Europe to promote his work. Even at the height of his fame he continued to provide concertos monthly for the Pietà, as his contract required him to do.

The Pietà was an orphanage, where wealthy Venetians placed their illegitimate daughters. It was run as a convent but it was essentially a musical conservatoire (one of four in the city). The girls received an excellent musical education. Although all the Venetian Ospedali taught string players, at the Pietà Vivaldi encouraged the playing of woodwind and brass instruments. There was plenty of time for practice and rehearsal. The standard of instrumental playing and its orchestra was renowned. Concerts were used as a means of raising money for the orphanage. Wealthy patrons enjoyed the spectacle of female instrumentalists (even if they were veiled or behind a screen).

Despite the quality of the musical education, the Ospedali did not turn out professional musicians. The men who played in Venice's orchestras and opera houses were privately trained and had passed an audition to belong to the Guild of Musicians. For a young woman at the Pietà the idea of a working life as a professional musician was out of the question: she was being educated for marriage. Those who did not marry stayed on as teachers, but the Pietà also employed male professional musicians as teachers.

The beginnings of the orchestra

Up to the mid-17th century there was no standard formation for the orchestra. The size of the orchestra and the numbers of each instrument varied regionally according to circumstances. Special occasions brought out ceremonial instruments such as trumpets and drums. In the opera house composers used woodwind instruments to accompany dancing, or occasionally in arias to add mood and atmosphere.

By the end of the 17th century the idea of a violin-dominated orchestra had caught on. Composers such as Lully in Paris and Corelli in Rome were writing for large numbers of strings, divided in parts, with a basso continuo. Pairs or groups of woodwind and brass were used, particularly for large concerts.

It was a golden age of violin making in northern Italy. Families of luthiers (craftsmen of stringed instruments) such as Stradivari and Guarneri developed the technology of violin making, producing instruments that had a brighter and more powerful tone. The gut strings were tightly strung to increase the volume. Italian players used a longer bow, suited to the singing-melodic style that the Italians adopted from operatic arias. Italian violins (and violinists) were exported throughout Europe. (The same luthiers also made violas, cello, basses and other stringed instruments that are no longer in regular use.)

Woodwind and brass instruments on the other hand were usually imported from France or Germany. Various instruments were in use as bass members of the reed family, with the bassoon emerging as the most commonly used. It had been developed successfully from the one-piece dulcian (a Renaissance double-reed instrument) into the four-jointed instrument that we know today. Unlike modern bassoons, early bassoons had very few keys. Bassoonists had to cover most of the notes with their fingers and probably only three keys. The early bassoon was versatile enough to play bass parts in a low register (with B♭ as its lowest note – three octaves below middle C) and higher melodies in the tenor range of the orchestra.

Basso continuo is Italian for 'continuous bass', sometimes known as 'through bass' or 'thoroughbass'. It was an essential feature of music in the 17th and 18th centuries. The bass line of the music was played by the bass instruments – usually a cello, double bass or a similar instrument such as the violone (a double bass viol, an ancestor of the double bass). The bassoon was also used as a continuo instrument.

The basso continuo

The continuo part was also played by a chordal instrument, usually a keyboard instrument such as a harpsichord or organ, or a plucked instrument such as a theorbo (a bass member of the lute family). The player was expected to 'realise' the bass, which meant adding chords to fit the harmonies of the bass and the rest of the ensemble. The basso continuo part often included numbers under the part – known as 'figured bass' – to identify the chord required. Players would frequently improvise by adding arpeggios or other figurations to fill out the texture. Realizing figured bass stylistically, using the correct harmonies, required much skill.

Modern editions of Vivaldi's music may include a realisation of the keyboard part, sometimes printed in smaller notes. This is only the editor's suggestion of how to interpret the figured bass. Experienced players have their own ideas of how to interpret a continuo.

> You are expected to compare different performances of the prescribed works. Listen out for differences in the realisation of the continuo. Are they simple or elaborate? Does the keyboard stay in the background or is it more prominent in places? Is there any extra melodic detail added or is it only chords?

Vivaldi and the concerto

The three-movement pattern (quick-slow-quick) became the usual structure for a concerto. Vivaldi wrote some concertos for pairs or groups of soloists (and also some without a soloist), but most of his c.500 concertos are for a single solo instrument. He wrote 39 bassoon concertos, more than for any other instrument – apart from the 230 violin concertos. While many of the violin concertos were published and became known throughout Europe, the bassoon concertos were not published. Their dates and origins are mostly unknown. For Vivaldi to write so many bassoon concertos suggests there may have been bassoon players at the Pietà who were capable of playing the demanding, virtuosic solo parts.

Ritornello form alternates a main theme for the orchestra (the ritornello) with sections for a soloist or a group of soloists (episodes). Sometimes the ritornello is called a 'tutti' (Italian for 'all') because

Ritornello form

The word 'ritornello' comes from the Italian *ritorno*, meaning 'return'.

everyone is playing. Vivaldi's development of ritornello form in the quick movements of the concertos set the pattern for many subsequent European composers.

Vivaldi gave his ritornellos memorable melodies and strong rhythms, establishing a clear sense of the tonic key at the beginning of the movement. Repeating the ritornello in related keys became important in the structure of the music. The music returned to the tonic in time for the final ritornello at the end of the movement. The solos were used to modulate between sections, to explore some ideas from the ritornello but also to introduce new, unrelated material.

Vivaldi experimented with different structural devices. His first solo sections were usually based on ideas from the opening ritornello. Elsewhere he could thematically link the solo and the ritornello. He experimented with different lengths of ritornello, perhaps based on only a short section of the original theme. Typically (but not in this prescribed orchestral work) the full theme would wait for the return of the tonic at the end of the movement. Such structural innovations (as well as Vivaldi's strong melodic style) influenced composers such as J. S. Bach, who arranged some of Vivaldi's concertos for keyboard. However, Bach and other European composers preferred the fuller restatements of the ritornellos, producing sections of more equal proportions.

Structure for the first movement

The structure of the first movement of Vivaldi's Bassoon Concerto in E minor, RV484, comprises four ritornellos and three solo sections. There are 27 bars for the orchestra and 40 bars for the soloist. The final solo is the longest of the episodes. There is no restatement of the full theme at the end: the concluding ritornello is only four bars long.

The 'RV' number used to identify Vivaldi's works refers to the catalogue by Peter Ryom, first published in 1973. Opus numbers were used for sets of his works that he had published during his lifetime.

One edition of this work counts the anacrusis (upbeat) as bar 1 and the first full bar as bar 2. For the purposes of this analysis the anacrusis bar is regarded as bar 0^4 and the first full bar as bar 1.

Bars	Section	Instrumentation	Length	Tonality
0^4–13^1	Ritornello 1	Full orchestra	12 bars	Tonic (E minor)
13–25^1	Solo 1	Bassoon + continuo violins	12 bars	
24^4–28^1	Ritornello 2	Full orchestra	3 bars	Dominant minor (B minor)
28^2–38^3	Solo 2	Bassoon + continuo	10½ bars	
38^2–46^1	Ritornello 3	Full orchestra	8 bars	Subdominant minor (A minor), modulating to tonic (E minor)
46^2–64^1	Solo 3	Bassoon + continuo violins	17½ bars	
64–67	Ritornello 4	Full orchestra	4 bars	Tonic (E minor)

Ritornello 1 (bars 0⁴–13¹)

The main theme of the movement is introduced in the second violins.

First idea ('a')

Bar 1 notates the A and F♯ at the beginning as appoggiaturas; bar 2 uses a fully written-out rhythm of a demisemiquaver on the stressed beat followed by a longer dotted semiquaver. This latter type of rhythm – known as a Lombardic rhythm or a Scotch snap – was a favourite of Vivaldi's. The use of the appoggiatura in this passage is discussed in detail on pages 64–65.

Some performers interpret the different notation of the rhythm by using the Lombardic rhythm in both bars. You may find varying approaches in different performances or even between the solo and orchestra in the same performance.

The first violins would normally have the melody. Instead they have a demisemiquaver accompaniment figure using arpeggiando bowing, which involves crossing three strings in one bow stroke. There are wide intervals between the notes of the chord because each note is played on a different string. This is a difficult figure to execute neatly, which may account for the reason why the melody and accompaniment are divided between the violins in this way.

The main melody is in the second violins. There is an accompaniment of repeated notes in the violas and continuo. This section of the theme comes to an end at bar 5 with triplet semiquavers in the melody against the continuing demisemiquavers in the first violins. Note the triple stopping in the first violins to give more emphasis to the loud E minor chord at bar 5³.

This melody is printed and discussed on pages 53–54, showing how Vivaldi develops single-bar phrases into a complete melody.

A secondary theme is introduced: a strong chord followed by a descending scale, played staccato, in octaves. Vivaldi often writes for the orchestra in octaves. It is a strong effect that brings out the melody and rhythm very clearly, and contrasts effectively with the harmonised sections of the music.

Second idea ('b')

Vivaldi contrasts the loud chord at bar 5³ with the soft, staccato scale that follows – which begins in a distinctive five-note rhythm in faster note values, the rest of the scale following in even quavers. The chord and scale are played three times, descending in a sequence through chords of B minor, A minor and E minor in first inversion (with G in the bass) before returning to the tonic. Note the use of the interval of the augmented 2nd in the minor scale (see bars 6¹ and 9²). The bass has an arpeggio figure to link the three phrases in descending sequence.

When you are writing about music, take care when using labels like 'a' and 'b'. An examiner will not know what you mean by 'a' or 'b' unless you first explain. Use a short description to link the music with your reference letter (or number) – for example, 'the opening legato melody' for 'a', 'the staccato descending scale idea' for 'b'.

Ritornello 1 concludes with the return of the 'a' melody for one bar, followed by a cadential figure that uses the faster-moving anacrusis figure and the quaver rhythm from the 'b' idea.

Solo 1 (bars 13–25[1])

The solo bassoon is accompanied by the continuo, often reduced in performances to a single cello and the realized harmony on the harpsichord (or another chord-playing instrument). The repeated quavers maintain the style of the ritornello through almost all of this solo section. The harmony changes twice a bar, on every minim beat.

The first solo section uses musical ideas from the opening ritornello, focusing on the 'a' material. The bassoon solo opens with the demisemiquaver arpeggios stated in the accompaniment for the opening theme. The arpeggios are in a closed formation, with the notes of the triad played as a broken chord. This is easier to play on the bassoon than the wide leaps of the violin version.

The violins answer the bassoon demisemiquavers in bars 14–16, using the triadic pattern of arpeggios. Both first and second violins play, with the seconds in harmony with the firsts. There is no slurred bowing marked. After the first answer in the violins at bar 14, the bassoon states for the first time the opening melody (bars 14[4]–16[3]). The first two phrases of the melody span nearly two octaves, with the second phrase descending to the bassoon's low E.

Vivaldi uses a descending sequence from bar 17 to bar 19, moving downwards through the circle of 5ths (see page 33 for more information on this device):

Bars	Chords (relating to key of E minor)	Chords (relating to transient keys)
17	ivb (A minor) – VII (D major)	vb – I (in D major)
18	IIIb (G major) – VI (C major)	Vb – I (in C major)
19	ii°b (F♯ diminished) – V (B major)	v°b – I (in B major – dominant key of E major)

Sequence was commonly used by composers of the Baroque period such as Vivaldi. Repeating a melodic figure sequentially was a good way of extending and developing a melodic phrase. The circle of 5ths pattern, with its strong-bass outline in the continuo, helps to drive the music forward and give it a sense of direction.

The modulation to the dominant key of B minor is established with a perfect cadence at bars 20–21. The harmonic rhythm varies at this point. Normally chords change every half bar, but at bar 21³ the harmony halts on an E minor chord (chord IV in the new key) for four beats while the bassoon plays a slower ascending chromatic figure. The rate of change in the harmony then speeds up towards the cadence in bars 24–25, making the change of key more emphatic. Only the bass (cello and keyboard) accompanies the bassoon, showing how important the continuo is to the music.

Look out for the virtuoso features of the bassoon line in bars 17–24:

➤ Rapid demisemiquaver arpeggios

➤ Wide leaps in the melody

➤ Trills

➤ Chromatic passages in a high register

➤ Rapid descending scale in demisemiquavers.

Most of the bassoon melody is in the higher register of the instrument, with the continuo providing a bass framework. Vivaldi also exploits the lowest register of the bassoon by using it as part of the bass. In the final full bar of the solo (bar 24) the bassoon decorates the bass line with the demisemiquaver broken chord figure and then a semiquaver figure which alternates the bass with the new tonic note B.

Ritornello 2 (bars 24⁴–28¹)

Vivaldi opts for a very short second ritornello, using the first two bars of the opening melodic 'a' idea and the final bar of the scalic 'b' material. With the contrasting key of B minor established, having a concise ritornello enables the soloist to continue with the solo as soon as possible.

The tonal scheme of the movement avoids major keys. The minor tonality of the main theme is preserved whenever the melody is repeated. Ritornello 2 is in the dominant minor (B minor); the third ritornello is in the subdominant minor (A minor). There is no ritornello in G major, the relative major, for example. Would having the melody in a major key alter the character of the movement?

Solo 2 (bars 28²–38³)

The bassoon immediately takes up the 'b' figure, which the orchestra has just played:

After this initial reference to the 'b' material, there follows newly developed material for this solo. The violins drop out completely for the second solo, leaving only the continuo accompaniment. The solo is free to explore ideas without direct reference to the ritornello material. The style of the accompaniment has changed too. While the first solo had used the repeated quavers of the 'a' material throughout, the continuo for the second solo is more varied:

Bars	Bassoon solo	Basso continuo
28–31^3	Descending scale figure from the 'b' section of the ritornello	Detached crotchets, separated by silences (as in the 'b' material from the ritornello). Followed by moving quavers for the cadence.
31^4–32	Descending sequence in demisemiquavers	Descending quavers on the crotchet beat, separated by rests. In 3rds with the bassoon.
33–38^3	New solo material	Consistent quaver movement, giving a sense of direction. Chords change every crotchet beat. Varied ways of keeping the bass movement going: passing notes, leaps between harmony notes, octave leaps.

The opening two bars of the melody (as in the example above of bars 28–29) are repeated a 3rd higher (bars 29^4–31^3). Underneath at this point there is a rapid change of chords at bars 30^3–31^3: from a D major chord, the bass moves up chromatically to D$\sharp$, followed by a dominant 7th chord (E^7) to modulate to A minor in bar 31. The music remains in this key for the rest of the solo.

The table shows the virtuoso features of the bassoon writing:

Opening statement of the melody	Bars 28–31^3
Movement between registers, wide leaps	7th or octave leaps: bars 29^1, 30^3, 35^1, 36^2 Larger leaps: 10ths in bar 31^3, 37^3; two octaves in bar 35$^{1-2}$
Demisemiquaver passagework	Descending sequence: bars 31^4–32 Descending scales: bar 36 (E to E, repeated); bar 37^2 (A natural minor)
Ornamentation	Trills: bars 29^2, 30^4, 31^2, 36^4, 38^2 Acciaccatura: bar 35$^{3-4}$
Decoration of the melodic line	Auxiliary note figure: bars 33^2, 33^4, 34^2, 34^4 Inverted auxiliary note figure: bar 35$^{3-4}$
Sustained melodic phrases, requiring control of breathing and expression	Bars 33–37^1, 37^2–38^3

Ritornello 3 (bars 38^2–46^1)

The orchestra returns with the ritornello theme in A minor; this is the longest of the ritornello restatements. The music quickly modulates to the tonic key of E minor at bar 41, by repeating the descending scale in the Lombardic rhythm over a dominant chord (bar 40).

The repetition of the 'b' material is similar to the opening ritornello, but the chords are slightly different. Compare bars 6–7 with bar 42: in the former, Vivaldi uses a dominant minor chord of B minor; in the latter, a major dominant chord of B major (with a sharpened leading note of D♯). The reason for the change from B minor to B major lies in the tonal structure of the movement. In the early part of the movement B minor is an important key centre; it is the key of the second ritornello. As we have seen, each repetition of the melody is in a minor key, so B minor is used for the second ritornello. Vivaldi's use of B minor in bar 6–7 prepares us for its use as a key centre there. However, at the end of the movement, the third ritornello employs the dominant major chord more freely to provide stronger harmony (suggesting a return to the tonic of E minor).

Solo 3 (bars 46²–64¹)

Solo 3, the longest of the solo sections, returns to the style of the first solo. Both make use of musical ideas from the 'a' part of the opening. The harmonic rhythm continues to be two chords per bar; and once again there is an accompanying role for the violins.

The solo begins with a new melodic idea, using repeated pairs of semiquavers.

The accompaniment in the first four bars (46–49) is for continuo only. The bassoon part has a range of more than two octaves, including a leap between the two extremes in bar 49. Most of the solo lies in the high tenor range of the instrument, with the lowest notes acting with the continuo as the bass.

The violins briefly interject with the demisemiquaver arpeggio figure from the first solo section (bar 50). The next two sections of bassoon solo are both sequences, each three bars long:

Bars	Solo	Accompaniment
50³–53³	Alternating demisemiquaver figure from Solo 1, with descending semiquaver broken chords	Continuo only. Violin demisemiquavers at the beginning (bar 50¹) and end (bar 53³). Falling circle of 5ths pattern: ➢ E minor – A minor ➢ D major – G major ➢ C major – F♯ dim/B⁷
54–57¹	Sequence with new material of triplet semiquavers	Continuo. Violins add repeated quavers and minim trills, alternating first and second violins. Suspension on the trilled notes: dissonant 7th added to the chord. Falling circle of 5ths pattern, with the richer sound of 7th chords: ➢ A minor – D⁷ ➢ G⁷ – C⁷ ➢ F♯ dim(+7) – B⁷ Violin demisemiquavers conclude.

The sequence at bars 54–57[1] is worth looking at closely for the sophisticated and highly expressive effect of its harmony and texture. The use of the trills in the violins is a particularly imaginative touch.

The violin demisemiquavers return for the final bars of the solo, interjecting in bar 61. The bassoon demisemiquavers in bars 61[3]–62 are an exact repeat of the beginning of the first solo (bars 13–14[2]). The concluding semiquaver pattern in bar 63 repeats the leaping semiquaver figure that ended the first solo (in bar 24), however, it is now stated in the tonic key.

Ritornello 4 (bars 64–67)

The brief tutti follows the earlier pattern of alternating 'a' and 'b' material. The final two bars repeat the octave unison figure as an echo: the first time *forte*; the second *piano*.

Vivaldi's reputation and influence

Further reading

The Birth of the Orchestra: History of an Institution 1650–1815 by John Spitzer and Neal Zaslaw. Oxford University Press, 2004, ISBN 978-0-19-816434-0.

Vivaldi by Michael Talbot (Master Musicians Series). Oxford University Press, 2000, ISBN 978-0-19-816497-5.

Vivaldi was very well known as a composer during his lifetime, but his reputation declined sharply after his death. Although 19th-century scholars were aware of his influence on J. S. Bach, it was only in the 1920s that Vivaldi's music was rediscovered in libraries and private collections in Italy. Scholars began to catalogue his works, which had previously been unknown. The Italian publishers Ricordi began printing a full edition of his instrumental works in the 1940s. Public performances and recordings of his work have made him one of the best known of Baroque composers. It is hard to believe that the most famous of his works, the four concertos called *The Four Seasons*, was completely unknown in the early part of the 20th century.

Exercise 24

1. Find two recordings of Vivaldi's Bassoon Concerto in E minor, and compare the first movement. Ideally, try to find one recording that uses period instruments. Listen out for the following points:

    ➤ **Ornamentation:** How do the performers interpret the ornaments in the printed score? What additional ornamentation is added by the performers?

    ➤ **Tempo change:** Can you hear the expressive use of rubato or phrasing in the solo bassoon part?

    ➤ **Instrumentation:** Compare the sound of the instruments – can you hear a difference between a modern-orchestral recording and one using period instruments?

    ➤ **Continuo harmony:** How does the continuo player realise the bass line? Which instruments are used?

2. Explain what is meant by ritornello form. How does Vivaldi make use of it?

3. What is the function of the basso continuo?

4. Describe briefly your understanding of audiences and the conditions for musicians in Venice during Vivaldi's lifetime.

Haydn: *Drum Roll* Symphony No. 103 in E♭, Hob. I:103

Joseph Haydn (1732–1809) wrote 12 symphonies for his two visits to London. Before travelling to London, Haydn spent most of his working life in service to the Esterházy family in Vienna and at their lavish summer palace of Eszterháza. Prince Nikolaus Esterházy kept a large musical establishment. As 'Kapellmeister' (director of music at the court) Haydn composed a huge quantity of music. He rehearsed and directed the court musicians in operas and orchestral music, written by himself and by other composers. He said that his isolation at Esterházy allowed him to experiment and forced him to become original.

Haydn's fame grew throughout Europe through the publication of his works and commissions such as his symphonies for Paris. By the 1790s he was the most famous composer in Europe. In London Haydn's works featured regularly in the subscription concert series of two rival orchestras, the Professional Concert and the Opera Concert. The venue for both series was the Hanover Square Rooms, a purpose-built concert hall, with a raised platform for the orchestra and room for an audience of more than 500 people.

In 1790 Johann Peter Salomon, violinist and leader of the Opera Concert, was in Europe looking for the best continental musicians for his orchestra. When he heard of the death of Prince Nikolaus Esterházy, he headed straight for Vienna to persuade Haydn to come to London.

There was a huge range of professional and amateur music in London. Although aristocratic patronage was important, England had a large middle class, made prosperous by the opportunities for business and industry in Britain and its overseas empire. For the price of an admissions ticket the English middle classes could enjoy the same entertainments as the aristocracy. Professional orchestras were a well-established feature of cultural life, playing in theatres, concert halls and in pleasure gardens, such as Vauxhall Gardens. Instrumental musicians – many of them from abroad – could make a good living working in a concert orchestra or in a theatre orchestra, supplementing their income by teaching or selling sheet music for a growing amateur market.

London was a new experience for Haydn. He made two visits between 1791 and 1795, and stayed for more than a year both times. He had little experience of foreign travel. The long and uncomfortable carriage journey from Vienna to London was a daunting prospect for a man of Haydn's age (now in his sixties). His visit to England is well documented from his letters, which show his interest and enthusiasm in everything he saw. Haydn was a popular and highly respected figure in England. He enjoyed the attention of English society, and he was proud of the honorary doctorate conferred on him by Oxford University.

Haydn's contracts with Salomon required him to produce six symphonies for each visit. At first he was at the forefront of the competition between the two subscription concerts. By the end of the second visit the orchestral scene had changed. Salomon's coup in securing Haydn for the Opera Concert had contributed to the

Franz Joseph Haydn is always known by his second name, Joseph.

Haydn did not number his symphonies systematically, nor were they published under opus numbers, unlike his string quartets for example. The listing of this work as No. 103 dates from the 1907 catalogue by publishers Breitkopf & Härtel, who had corresponded with Haydn on the subject a hundred years earlier.

'Hob. I:103' refers to the first section (the Symphonies) of Anthony van Hoboken's catalogue (3 volumes, 1957, 1971, 1978), which preserves the Breitkopf & Härtel numbers.

failure and winding up of the rival Professional Concert season. Many of its players joined Salomon's orchestra. Haydn's last three symphonies – including No. 103 – were written for an enlarged orchestra of about 60 players. The venue for the concerts was the King's Theatre, where a concert room seating 800 people had been built at the back of the stage.

The *Drum Roll* Symphony

Many of Haydn's symphonies have nicknames, some of them related to the musical characteristics of the work. The *Drum Roll* Symphony (in German 'Paukenwirbel') takes its name from the timpani roll at the beginning of the first movement. The London audience would have found this a striking and novel effect.

Haydn's earlier symphonies were typically in three movements and written for strings, oboes and horns. This symphony is on the larger scale of his later symphonies. There are four movements. The first movement has a slow introduction, which adds seriousness and scale to the symphony. The second movement is a variation on two folksong melodies, with a violin solo for the leader of the orchestra. (At the first performance by the Opera Concert this solo would have been played by G. B. Viotti, who had taken over from Salomon as leader of the orchestra.) The third movement is a minuet. The fourth movement (prescribed work) adopts sonata rondo form.

The first performance took place on 2 March 1795. (It was played again later in the concert series.) No. 103 was the penultimate symphony that Haydn composed for London. The last symphony (No. 104) is known as the *London* Symphony. Confusingly 'London Symphonies' is used to refer to the whole series of 12 symphonies Nos 93–104; they are also sometimes called the 'Salomon symphonies'.

Haydn's orchestra in London

The orchestra uses two of each woodwind instrument – a double wind orchestra – and also two trumpets, two horns and a pair of timpani. The flutes play in unison (they divide into first and second in the slow movement, but not in the rest of the symphony) and give a bright sound at the top of the ensemble range. Clarinets were a new feature for Haydn: only the last three of his symphonies employ them.

Modern-valved brass instruments had not been invented yet, so the horns and trumpets could only play a limited number of pitches – the notes of the harmonic series. The term 'natural' (natural horn, natural trumpet) is used to mean this type of brass instrument. If you look through the horn and trumpet parts in the fourth movement you will see which notes were available. There are more notes at the higher end of the range, but not a complete scale, which limits the use of the brass if the music modulates away from the tonic key. Symphony No. 103 is in E♭ major, so the horns and trumpets are crooked in E♭. A horn player in Haydn's time (and in Beethoven's) would have been equipped with a set of about nine crooks, detachable lengths of tubing with which it would be possible to extend or shorten the playing length of the instrument.

There was a different length crook for each key that the player was likely to need. Below are some key points to remember about the brass instruments in this symphony:

> The written note C sounds as E♭

> Horns in E♭ sound a major 6th lower than written

> Trumpets in E♭ sound a minor 3rd higher.

See pages 74–75 for more on transposing brass instruments.

Haydn played the piano in performances of his 'London Symphonies', but in general the idea of a basso continuo was dying out. The continuo was in use for recitatives in opera and vocal music, but as the orchestra got larger – with chords fully arranged for sections of woodwind or brass – a chord-playing keyboard instrument was no longer needed to support the harmonic structure in symphonies. Modern performances, even ones in 'period' style, tend to leave out any supporting keyboard.

The fourth movement (sonata rondo form)

For Haydn and Mozart the last movement (the *finale*) of a sonata or symphony was usually a lively, dance-like piece. Light and undemanding (earlier movements required more concentration from the audience), it usually made for a tuneful end to the work. The *Drum Roll* Symphony ends with a fast movement in what we now call sonata rondo form. This form combines elements of rondo form with sonata form, producing a hybrid version of the two.

Both Haydn and Mozart often used rondo form for their *finales*, alternating principal sections (A) with contrasting episodes: ABACADA(Coda). The episodes in a rondo could be used to bring in a change of mood – a minor key, some contrapuntal writing, a new theme, and so on.

Sonata form is sometimes called 'first movement form', because that was where it was most often used. Sonata form usually takes the following structure:

Section	Themes / material	Key centre
Exposition	First subject Second subject	Tonic Dominant
Development	(Exposition material developed)	Other (related) keys
Recapitulation	First subject Second subject	Tonic
(Coda)		

A 'subject' is a theme or group of themes. In sonata form the two subjects represent two different key areas.

For composers the dramatic and expressive possibilities of sonata form lay in using contrasting themes for the first and second subjects, and in the use of tonality. In the development the exposition material could be replayed and modified in new keys. The return to the tonic key for the recapitulation (the repeat of material from the beginning) was an important moment in the music. In a rondo form the main theme (the principal section A) returns a few times, usually in the tonic key.

As a hybrid of sonata and rondo form, Haydn's *finale* combines features of both:

➢ A sonata form in which the first subject returns in the tonic before the development

➢ A rondo form with a long opening section; it concludes with an episode section instead of the rondo theme.

The movement is also monothematic: there is only one main theme. You can see this if you compare the main theme (first subject) at bars 5–8 with the episode (second subject) at bars 110–113. The melodies are the same, but Haydn creates variety by using different keys, instrumentation and phrasing. Listen to how the two melodies are differently placed in relation to the regular four-bar phrases in the music. The strongest natural accents are at bar 5^1 and at bar 111^1.

This movement is a fine example of Haydn's experimentation with form. From his Eszterháza years he had been used to trying things out to see if they would work. For the London audience Haydn's genius lay in his ability to develop simple musical material in an imaginative and intellectual way. It was these qualities that led English newspaper reports of the time to refer to Haydn as 'the Shakespeare of music'.

Structural analysis The table that follows gives a detailed overview of the fourth movement:

Rondo form	Tonality	Themes		Sonata form
A Theme (1–107)	TONIC E♭ major modulates to DOMINANT	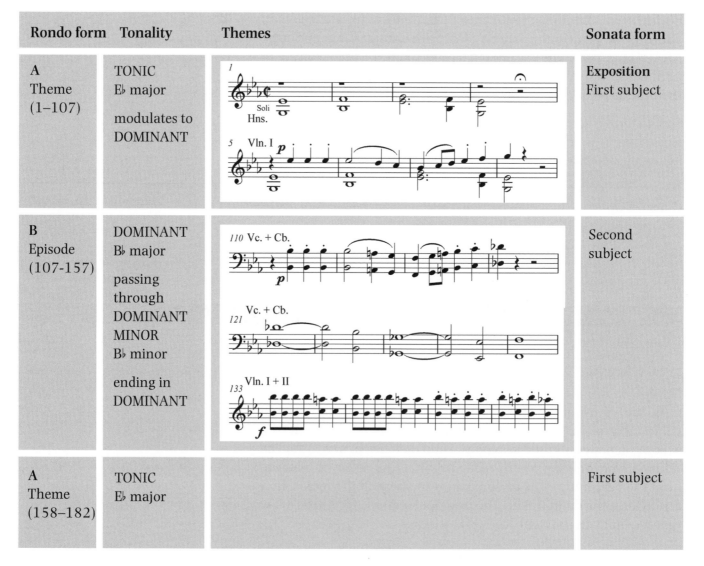		**Exposition** First subject
B Episode (107–157)	DOMINANT B♭ major passing through DOMINANT MINOR B♭ minor ending in DOMINANT			Second subject
A Theme (158–182)	TONIC E♭ major			First subject

Rondo form	Tonality	Themes	Sonata form
C Episode (182–263)	RELATIVE MINOR C minor modulating to D♭ major then to F minor back to D♭ major ending on a G major chord (V in C minor)	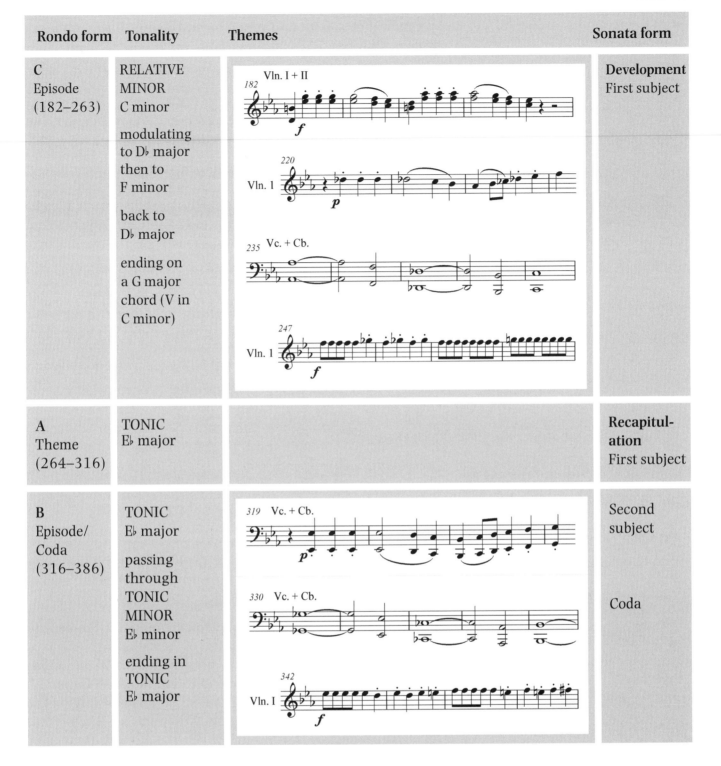	**Development** First subject
A Theme (264–316)	TONIC E♭ major		**Recapitulation** First subject
B Episode/ Coda (316–386)	TONIC E♭ major passing through TONIC MINOR E♭ minor ending in TONIC E♭ major		Second subject Coda

Exercise 25

1. How does Haydn use tonality to structure the music of this movement? How does this compare with the use of tonality in the first movement of Vivaldi's Bassoon Concerto in E minor?

2. How has the orchestra, as used by Haydn, changed from the time of Vivaldi?

3. In what ways was writing for a London audience different from what Haydn was used to?

The theme

The main theme in the violins is derived from a Croatian folk song. The horn call at the start of the movement (bars 1–4) is repeated in bars 5–8 so that the first violin phrase appears to be a countermelody to the horns. The second phrase (bars 9–12), played by the first and second violins, begins in 3rds and is accompanied by the clarinets; this phrase modulates to the dominant key, B♭ major.

This full version of the theme – with its horn countermelody – is heard five times in the fourth movement. Each time it is in the tonic key of E♭ major. The first three appearances are in the opening section (the exposition):

➤ Bars 5–12: opening theme

➤ Bars 45–52: exact repeat of the opening

➤ Bars 73–76: full orchestra, first phrase only, theme in the lower parts.

The other two appearances are at the repeats of the A section:

➤ Bars 158–165: exact repeat of opening

➤ Bars 264–271: exact repeat of opening.

The episodes (sections B and C of the rondo form) use the first phrase (bars 5–8) only.

Section A – the theme (bars 1–107)

The horn call at the start of the movement is a call to attention. Haydn has no dynamic markings for the horns but this is usually played loudly. After a short pause the horn call is repeated, now as an important part of the main theme.

Almost immediately Haydn breaks down the violin theme into motifs. A motif is a small section of a melody that has a recognisable identity. Composers often highlight a particular feature of pitch, rhythm or harmony to characterise the motif. Repeating or developing a motif is a common way of driving the music on while bringing a sense of unity to the piece. The rhythm and repeated notes of Haydn's theme give the movement much of its intensity and rhythmic momentum.

At bars 12–15 the lower and upper strings exchange a motif from the opening notes of the second phrase (first stated in bars 9–12[1]), briefly passing through F minor. The passage is repeated a tone lower (ending with a perfect cadence in the tonic), but rearranged for the violins. The motif is shortened further at bars 18–20:

Compare the opening of the fourth movement of Haydn's *Drum Roll* Symphony with other works that use similar repeated figures, including the first movement of Beethoven's Violin Concerto (see pages 99–110). Look also at the use of motifs in jazz, for example in Duke Ellington's *Koko* (see pages 136–141).

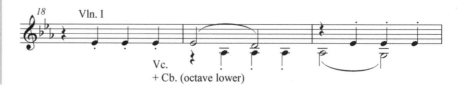

In the opening section, Theme A (exposition), Haydn keeps the audience waiting until bar 73 for the full orchestra to play. The woodwind and brass are used very sparingly and not as full sections

– horns, clarinets, oboes and bassoon are used separately in pairs or as a solo on sustained notes.

A series of long sustained notes contributes to the building up of suspense. Such notes are known as pedal notes, in this case a dominant pedal of B♭ (the dominant note of E♭ major). The table below traces the use of pedal notes and motifs:

Bars	Pedal note	Use of motifs
18–25	➤ Oboe ➤ Inverted pedal (because it is not the lowest note in the texture)	➤ The melody in two-bar motifs ➤ Imitation (antiphony) between first violins and lower strings ➤ Repeated an octave higher ➤ Leading to descending sixths in oboe and violins ➤ Modulating to dominant (B♭ major)
28–39	➤ Double basses ➤ Double bass part is independent of the cellos ➤ Detached minims at the end in both cellos and basses	➤ Uses the repeated note anacrusis ➤ Extends the descending legato second bar with an ascending bar ➤ Imitation between first violins and violas/cellos ➤ Exact repetition (canon), but violins are a tone higher (canon at the 2nd) ➤ Cellos double the melodic line with the violas
39–44	➤ Bassoon ➤ Bass pedal in a higher register	➤ Motif is now reduced to the three repeated notes ➤ Lighter texture (strings and bassoon only) ➤ Rising chromatic chords
57–61	➤ 2 oboes ➤ Inverted pedal ➤ In octaves to match the fuller string texture	➤ Two-bar motif ascends (an inversion of the original motif) ➤ Full strings, violins in octaves

At bar 65 – just as the audience believes a tutti is surely about to occur – the texture is reduced to three parts, with violins and violas exchanging staccato repeated notes. The quiet dynamics increase the impact of the forte in the full orchestra when it finally arrives at bar 73.

Only the first phrase of the main theme is stated at the tutti, this time in clarinets, bassoons, violas and cellos. The violins, flutes and oboes (reinforced by horns, trumpets and drums) play the horn call from the opening of the movement. This has been modified, with faster rhythmic movement and with a change of harmony.

As the music begins to modulate to B♭ major, the theme is extended by using motifs from the main theme (compare with the legato phrases at bars 28–34). The texture becomes imitative as Haydn exchanges the two-bar motif between various instruments. He also adds other strands to create a rich polyphonic texture.

Listening Listen to a recording of the fourth movement while following the score. Listen out for some of the following details:

➤ Bar 76: theme in the bass (cellos, double basses, bassoons), developing into an ascending scale to the high F pedal at bar 82

➤ Rapid exchange of motifs at different pitches: bar 81 (oboes, starting on G); bar 82 (first violins/flutes, starting on C); bar 83 (second violins/clarinets, starting on D)

➤ The motif harmonised in 3rd or 6ths in another part: bar 76 (violas, an octave and a 6th above the bass); bar 83 (oboes, in 3rds with the second violins and clarinets)

➤ Suspensions in inner parts: bars 79–81 (the F in the second violins, followed by E♭ and D)

➤ Bars 82–90: the exchange of the repeated-note motif in the horns, also played an octave higher in the trumpets.

The F pedal that begins at bar 82 is a dominant pedal in the new key of B♭ major. Note the *forzando* (a strong accent) on the dissonant chord (bar 86) formed by the D and E♮ on the strong beat. This is an exuberant passage in which the first and second violins imitate the motif. A new accompanying descending scale figure at bar 91 leads to a homophonic conclusion of this section. The harmonic rhythm slows to a chord every two bars for the *fortissimo* at bar 101.

Exercise 26

1. Compare the music before and after each appearance of the theme (bars 5–12, 45–52, 158–165, 264–271). Describe what happens.

2. Write out the cello and viola parts in bars 73–76[1] in the treble clef.

3. Explain how a motif is different from a theme.

4. Describe some of the orchestral textures that Haydn uses in this movement.

5. What is meant by the term sonata rondo form?

Section B – the first episode (or second subject) (bars 107–157)

After the climax of the opening section, the pace of the B section is less hectic. The melodic activity of the strings is replaced by repeated crotchets. The dynamic marking is *piano* and the texture reduces to strings with occasional woodwind. The harmonic rhythm slows: four bars for the first chord (I in the new dominant key of B♭ major), then alternating I and V^7 every two bars, with one chord per bar at the cadences (see bars 125–126 and 131–132).

The episode has three melodic ideas (see the examples in the structural analysis table on page 92). Note the contrast in the use of the minor key and the legato cellos and basses at bars 121–132. With the return of the major key in the full orchestra at bar 133, the harmonic rhythm increases suddenly to two chords per bar, and up to four chords in a bar (in bars 135–138). Note the examples of double stopping in the violins (bars 141–142) followed by triple stopping in the subsequent two bars, which add emphasis to the cadential chords.

The link passage in bars 146–157 brings the music back to the tonic, using a pedal B♭ under shifting chromatic chords until a dominant 7th chord is reached.

Return of the theme (bars 158–182)

Following the first episode, the main theme returns in a shortened form of only 25 bars. This statement is almost identical to the first appearance of the theme at bars 5–26, with the exception of an inverted motif in the clarinet at bar 172.

Section C – the second episode (or development) (bars 182–263)

A development section in sonata form often explores the exposition material in new keys. If you refer back to the structural analysis chart on page 92 you will notice that after the opening C minor section, the rest of the C episode follows a similar path to the two B sections. The second subject material appears in the same order. However, it is now developed to explore more adventurous tonality.

The use of the relative minor key of C minor makes the motivic imitation more urgent and dramatic. The overlap of the exchanges of the two-bar motif makes the repeated note figure appear in almost every bar. Some of the entries of the motif are harmonised in 3rds, played by different combinations of strings and woodwind, creating a chordal string texture to the section.

The development shows some of the limitation of brass and timpani in keys that are more distant from the tonic, even the relative minor. The brass section is able to support by reinforcing the rhythm of the repeated notes on G and E♭, but C (written as A) is not available. The timpani's E♭ and B♭ are not much use in C minor but the E♭ is available for the E♭ major passage in bar 190.

The flexibility of the classical style allows Haydn to change moods quickly. At bar 198 he changes to soft upper strings, playing a legato version of the motif in even crotchets. The full orchestra returns at bar 208, with sudden syncopated accents (marked *forzando*) dispersed over the following five bars. The harmonies change on the syncopated beats, emphasising the feeling of disruption. The music has moved suddenly to the distant key of D♭ major. The *fortissimo* full orchestra (with brass and timpani) marks the perfect cadence at bars 215–217.

The development section continues to explore the material from the episode. There are some differences in the treatment of the material. In this section the first violins lead with the melody, answered by the cellos and basses. There is a change of key to F minor for the repeat. The legato theme, which was previously repeated in the cellos and basses in the same key, is now answered in the violins – with gentle woodwind chords as the music returns to D♭ major. The section ends with a G major chord (bar 263) as if preparing to continue in C minor.

Recapitulation (bar 264–end)

Having built up the suspense, Haydn surprises us with an abrupt return to the tonic key. The first-subject material of the first 107 bars is repeated, now compressed into 53 bars (bars 264–316). The theme is played once, in the same scoring as before, but for the recapitulation there is no long build up to a repeat of the main theme. As before there is a brief modulation to the dominant over the B♭ pedal (bars 287–299), which now incorporates added bassoons, trumpets, horns and timpani to match the full orchestra. The music reverts immediately to the tonic (bar 300), which will be the key of the repeat of the B section and the end of the movement.

After the second-subject material (bars 316–350) there is a brief coda to bring the movement to a rousing conclusion. The rapid, leaping violin writing in the final tutti (bar 368 onwards) gives an idea of the virtuosity that Haydn expected from his London musicians. The high G in the violinist's 6th position (bar 379–383) is unusual in orchestral writing at this time, although common in solo violin music.

Haydn's original manuscript for this score has a different ending (bars 338–end); the ending that is usually played today was added to the score. Both versions of the ending are usually printed in the editions available of the score. The original ending can be heard on the CD *Haydn: The London Symphonies, Vol. 1* by Frans Brüggen and the Orchestra of the 18th Century (Universal Classics).

Further reading

Haydn edited by David Wyn Jones (Oxford Composer Companions). Oxford University Press, 2002, ISBN 978-0-19-955452-2.

Haydn: A Creative Life in Music by Karl Geiringer (3rd edition). University of California, 1992, ISBN 978-0-52-004317-6.

Exercise 27

1. Make an analysis chart to show the differences between the tonality, themes and instrumentation of the B and C sections of this movement.

2. Listen to performances of this movement by different orchestras and conductors. Compare a performance from 50 years ago with a modern performance or with one that uses 'period' instruments.

Beethoven: Violin Concerto in D major, Op.61

In 1792 Ludwig van Beethoven (1770–1827) arrived in Vienna from the German town of Bonn to have lessons with Joseph Haydn. An accomplished pianist and composer, the young Beethoven was already identified as a 'second Mozart'. There was a plan for Haydn to take him to London, but that did not come off, and Haydn passed his teaching duties to others.

Vienna, the largest German-speaking city of the time, was the capital of the Austro-Hungarian Empire. Ruled by the Habsburg family, it was the centre of an imperial bureaucracy that controlled a large part of Europe. Its opportunities attracted musicians from all over Europe, particularly from Italy and Germany. The imperial court promoted church, opera, dance and instrumental music. There were no regular subscription concerts as Haydn had found in London, but patronage by the nobility was an important force in the cultural life of Vienna. Wealthy aristocratic families cultivated the playing and composing of instrumental music as a sign of their noble status and education. The popularity of instrumental music also increased among the middle classes, creating a new market for published music.

Beethoven began to make a successful career for himself in Vienna. Many of his performances and compositions were for private concerts for aristocratic society. He gave lessons to various members of the nobility and accepted commissions from aristocrats (to whom most of his works were dedicated). Unusually the Violin Concerto in D major is dedicated to Beethoven's friend Stephan von Breuning. Beethoven was also a shrewd businessman when it came to the publication of his music. He made an arrangement of the concerto for piano and orchestra (known as Op. 61a) as part of a contract with the English publisher (and composer) Clementi to publish his works in London. This arrangement is dedicated to von Breuning's wife, Julie.

Beethoven composed more slowly than either Vivaldi or Haydn. Even allowing for the large scale of his works, his total of nine symphonies and seven published concertos seems very little in comparison to Haydn's hundred symphonies or Vivaldi's five hundred concertos. Beethoven's method of composition involved notebooks of ideas, sketches in which melodies were drafted and redrafted until he was satisfied.

The Violin Concerto in D major was written for violinist Franz Clement, whose playing Beethoven admired. Clement had appeared in London with both Haydn (on Haydn's first visit) and Salomon. Returning to Vienna he became the conductor at the new Theater an der Wien, where the first performance of Beethoven's concerto took place on 23 December 1806. The occasion was a benefit concert (a concert to raise money for a particular cause); in this case the beneficiary was Clement himself. A benefit concert was a useful way for musicians to supplement their income at a time when they were not well paid. The orchestra for Clement's benefit concert was made up of available players, giving their services for free to help a fellow musician.

The solo violin part reflects Clement's qualities as a player. He was known for his elegant, lyrical style of playing, using the shorter Italian bow rather than the new, longer Tourte bow. Beethoven made various changes to the violin part in response to suggestions from Clement. The performance was not a great success. Clement performed it again at other times in his career. However, like many of Beethoven's major works, it was slow to gain public acceptance. In 1844 the violinist Joseph Joachim performed the concerto at the age of 12 in London with the composer Felix Mendelssohn conducting. This was the beginning of the growth of the concerto's popularity.

The violin

Major advances in violin technology at this time brought more power and brilliance to the sound of the violin. The neck was lengthened, increasing the sounding length of the strings. Longer strings meant slightly more room between the notes, making playing in the highest registers more practical. In the first movement of Beethoven's Violin Concerto in D major, the solo part goes up to a top E (bar 204), two octaves above the open E string. In Paris, François Tourte developed the modern bow, which was curved inwards (by heating the stick and then bending it into shape), balanced, used more bowhair and had more weight at the frog (bottom) end of the bow.

Beethoven's style

The first movement of the violin concerto uses wide contrasts. The style is predominantly lyrical, with understated, quiet woodwind themes and a highly expressive, melodic solo violin part. In contrast the full orchestra is used at a *fortissimo* dynamic early in the work (bar 28) and then at regular intervals throughout. *Sforzandi* are used for powerful accents, even in the loudest passages. Modern performances usually use a larger orchestra for Beethoven's works than for Haydn's, but the orchestra has almost the same list of instruments as Haydn's *Drum Roll* Symphony. Apart from the use of one flute, it is a double wind orchestra. Haydn's London orchestra was unusually large compared to Viennese orchestras.

The wide range of dynamics and the dramatic use of crescendos, diminuendos, sudden changes of dynamics and accents are part of a trend in early 19th-century music (and in art and literature). These trends signalled a move towards more obvious expression of feeling or emotion, known as the 'Romantic' movement. The larger orchestra – increasingly dominated by professional players, with a fully functioning woodwind section – allowed composers to achieve a great variety of expressive effects through different orchestration techniques (combining instruments in different ways).

The role of the orchestra

The woodwind section has an important role to play in the first movement:

➢ The flute, oboes, clarinets and bassoons contrast in timbre with the sound of the solo violin and with the string section

➢ Important themes are introduced by the woodwind section

➢ The woodwind can either play themes as a full section or play melodic lines in unison, octaves, 3rds, 6ths accompanied by strings

➤ Woodwind instruments are used as a section in homophonic writing, reinforcing the rhythm in the full orchestra or holding a chord while the strings play a more energetic rhythmic figure

➤ The woodwind can be used to strengthen melodic lines by doubling the strings

➤ The bassoon is used for expressive effect in dialogue with the solo violin in the development (both bassoons in 3rds, bars 305–327) and in the coda.

There are two horns and two trumpets, crooked to play in D major (see page 90 for an explanation of 'crooked'). The timpani are tuned to D and A, the tonic and dominant. As in Haydn's *Drum Roll* Symphony, the brass and timpani add extra weight to the sound of the full orchestra, but they are also used in quieter passages. Below are two examples of how the timpani and wind section are employed for expressive effects:

➤ The opening unaccompanied timpani motif – the five crotchet notes in the first two bars – is an important thematic idea that returns throughout the movement

➤ The passage in the development section (bar 330 onwards) includes an extended violin solo. This is accompanied by *pianissimo* horns, which are playing the opening timpani motif in octaves. The same motif is then taken up by the bassoons at bar 338 (substituting for brass because B♭ is not available to crooked instruments), and then by trumpets and timpani together (bars 346–357).

| **Exercise 28** |

Make a chart to show the different uses of the woodwind in the first movement of Beethoven's Violin Concerto in D major. Find an example in the score for the first five bullet points listed in 'The role of the orchestra' section above. (The sixth bullet point – the bassoon in the coda – has been found for you).

The first movement

At 535 bars in total, the first movement of the Violin Concerto in D major is one of the longest of Beethoven's first movements. Some of its structural features are typical of sonata form (see page 91). In common with the usual pattern in a concerto, the traditional repeat of the exposition is written out in full with the solo part added, known as the solo exposition. Beethoven was also influenced by the French violin concertos of the period, which typically used four ritornellos and three solo sections within the first movement.

The first movement can be discussed in terms of sonata form or as a structure of alternating ritornellos and solos. The table that follows gives a summary of the overall structure, tonality and themes. The musical examples are 'incipits' – the opening bars only. These are a reminder of how each sonata form section begins, so not all the themes are included. The opening material of the second

'Tutti' means 'all' or 'everyone'. It can be used to mean the full orchestra, when all instruments are playing. In discussing a concerto the term tutti can also be used to mean any section of the music when the orchestra is playing but not the soloist. This is why some scores print the word 'Tutti' in bar 1, marking the beginning of an orchestral section in the movement.

If you are using this chart to help you revise for the exam, think about what you can remember and about what an examiner will want to know from you:

1. The fact or statement you want to make

2. Location of the evidence: a brief description (bar numbers are difficult to remember)

3. The evidence: a brief description of the music.

Combining these three points into a single paragraph allows you to be clear and specific in your answer. For example:

"The bassoon is used for expressive effect in dialogue with the solo violin (Point 1). In the coda (Point 2) the closing theme from the exposition is played by the bassoon. Previously the theme was played loudly by the full orchestra, but instead the coda has the melody in the solo bassoon in a high register over sustained *pianissimo* chords in the strings, with more elaborate answering phrases in the solo violin (Point 3)."

subject in the exposition (bars 43–46), the solo exposition (bars 144–147) and recapitulation (bars 418-421) is also given.

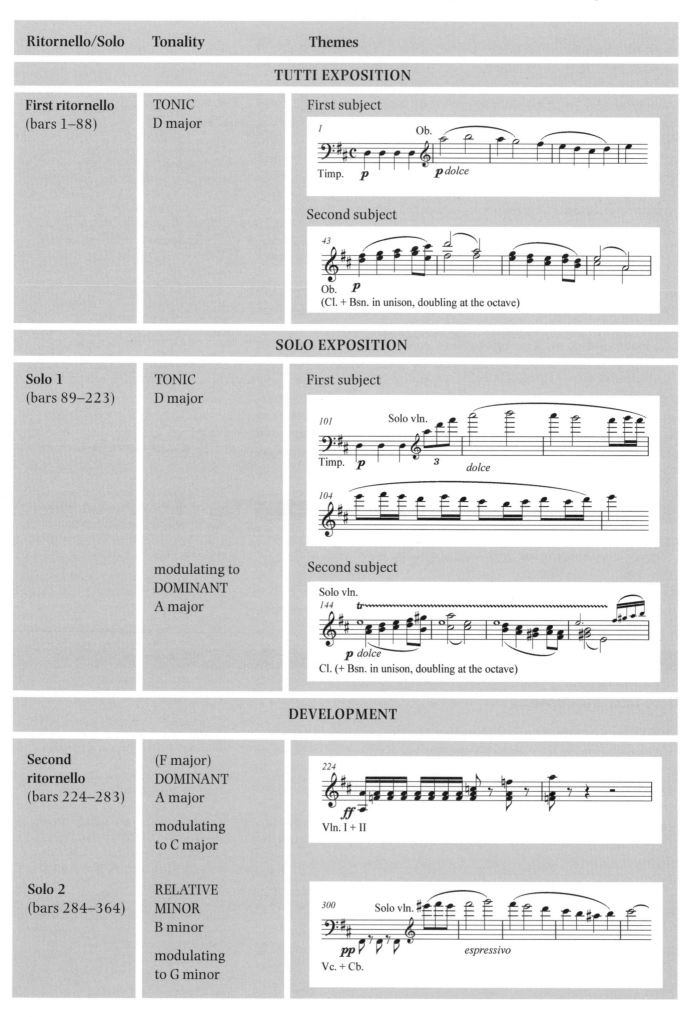

Ritornello/Solo	Tonality	Themes
TUTTI EXPOSITION		
First ritornello (bars 1–88)	TONIC D major	First subject Second subject (Cl. + Bsn. in unison, doubling at the octave)
SOLO EXPOSITION		
Solo 1 (bars 89–223)	TONIC D major modulating to DOMINANT A major	First subject Second subject Cl. (+ Bsn. in unison, doubling at the octave)
DEVELOPMENT		
Second ritornello (bars 224–283)	(F major) DOMINANT A major modulating to C major	
Solo 2 (bars 284–364)	RELATIVE MINOR B minor modulating to G minor	

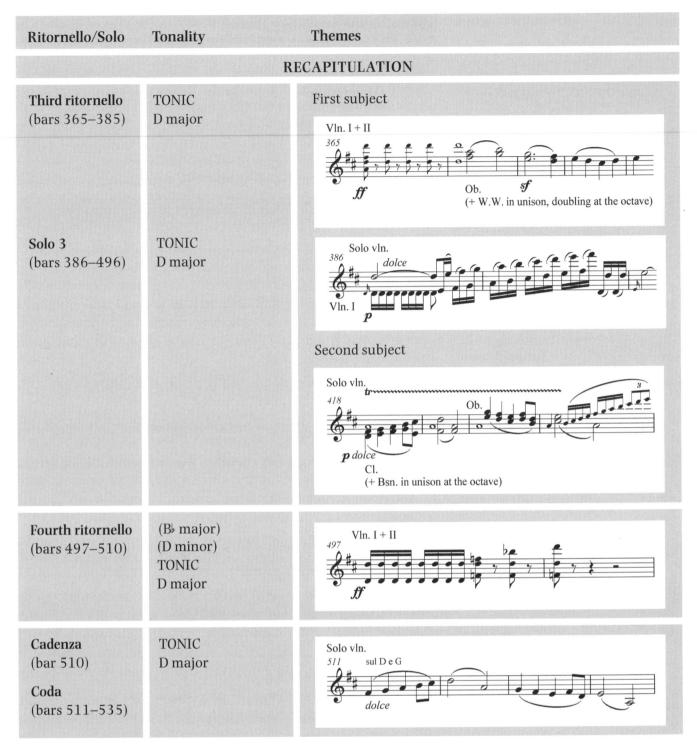

Ritornello/Solo	Tonality	Themes
	RECAPITULATION	
Third ritornello (bars 365–385)	TONIC D major	First subject
Solo 3 (bars 386–496)	TONIC D major	Second subject
Fourth ritornello (bars 497–510)	(B♭ major) (D minor) TONIC D major	
Cadenza (bar 510) **Coda** (bars 511–535)	TONIC D major	

Tutti exposition

Beethoven lays out the main material for the movement in the exposition. Usually we talk of sonata form expositions as having a first subject (in the tonic) followed by a second subject (in the dominant key). 'Subject' is just another word for a melody or a phrase or some other musical idea. It would be easy to assume that a 'first subject' consists only of a single musical idea. In practice composers tend to use more than one idea. The terms 'first subject group' and 'second subject group' more accurately show that there can be more than one theme.

First subject group

First subject group		
1a	bar 1	Timpani motif and opening woodwind theme
1b	bar 10	Strings take up timpani motif, beginning on D♯
1c	bar 18	Woodwind ascending scales idea, with repeated semiquavers in the strings
1d	bar 28	Full orchestra motif (*fortissimo*) based on repeated semiquaver rhythm, unexpected B♭ major chord
1e	bar 35	Five-note semiquaver figure, accents on second and fourth beats

Timpani motif

The five repeated crotchets in the timpani in bars 1–2 are more than just an introduction to the woodwind melody. This rhythmic motif is used in many places within the first movement, giving a sense of unity to the music. In the exposition this motif links the different melodic ideas:

➢ In bar 10 the motif is used for the first appearance of the strings. The chromatic note of D♯ contrasts strongly with the diatonic harmonies (emphasising chords I and V) in the opening woodwind theme

➢ Modified versions of the motif are found in the rhythms of the 1c and 1d material

➢ The motif is used to accompany the second subject theme. The chromatic version (1b) also reappears.

Second subject group

Second subject group		
2a	bar 43	Woodwind theme in two-bar phrases: ascending 3rds, answered by descending 3rds, pizzicato cellos and double basses. 'Timpani motif' in the first violins, notated as quavers.
2b	bar 51	Minor key version of 2a in violins (in octaves), triplet quavers throughout in violas and cellos. Motif in horns, trumpets and timpani.
1b	bar 65	Chromatic D♯ motif from 'First subject group', building from *pp* to *ff*. The motif is in full strings (*pianissimo*), harmonised as a diminished 7th chord.
2c	bar 77	Tutti closing theme, alternating two-bar phrases for violins (chord I) and cellos and double basses (chord V).

A diminished 7th chord is a chromatic chord built up of minor 3rds. At bar 65 the notes are F♯, A, C, D♯. It is often used in dramatic or expressive contexts, for example the sforzando chords in bars 209–213 of Haydn's Symphony No. 103.

Exercise 29

Look at how the timpani motif is used later in the movement at the following points:

➢ Towards the end of the first violin solo (bars 205–223)

➢ The second half of the development (bars 300–364)

➢ The beginning of the recapitulation (bars 365–381).

Tonality

The first and second subject woodwind themes (bars 2–5 and 43–46, respectively) are similar in character. They are diatonic, using only the notes in the major key. The harmonies are based on alternating tonic and dominant chords. The rhythm and phrasing is very similar: crotchets and minims, grouped in clear phrases of two or four bars.

In common with the usual practice in concertos, there is no modulation to the dominant key in the tutti exposition (that occurs in the solo exposition). The second subject begins and ends in the tonic. Contrasting with the diatonic harmonies of the woodwind, the strings have a more chromatic role, disturbing the D major tonality with the D♯ version of the timpani motif (1b).

The first entry of the full orchestra at bar 28 on the chord of B♭ major is a surprising and dramatic effect. It is harmonically surprising because it is distant from D major: the precise relationship is that it is the flattened submediant (a tertiary-key relation to the tonic).

The 1e material at bar 35 alternates dominant and tonic minor (D minor) chords. The semiquaver motif in the unaccompanied first violins at bars 39–41 changes the F♮ to F♯ to prepare for the return back to D major.

The move to the tonic minor is even clearer in the second subject at bar 51, where the violin version of the woodwind theme is in D minor. The melody is extended by a brief modulation to F major (bars 57–58). The melody and chords are repeated in sequence a 3rd lower (in bars 59–60), returning to the key of D minor. The sequence is repeated as the music grows in volume, with the melody now harmonised in 3rds by the woodwind.

Exercise 30

In Section B of the listening exam you have to answer questions on a short passage from one of the prescribed orchestral works. You may be asked about the chords, keys and cadences in the passage. You will have a copy of the score to help you and you will be able to listen to a recording.

1. In your Beethoven score, look at the passage from bar 19 to bar 42. It begins in D major, the tonic key of the movement. There are no accidentals (sharps, flats or naturals) until bar 28, where there is a chord of B♭ major. Find the notes of this chord (B♭, D and F) in the score:

   ➢ The bass notes are usually in the cellos, basses and bassoons

   ➢ Other notes of the chord can be found in the treble clef instruments – in the violins, flute and oboes

> ➢ If you are still not sure, work out the notes in the transposing instruments (clarinets, horns and trumpets) or the violas (in the alto clef).

To work out the key or tonality of a passage, you need to look at a few bars – compare the notes in the score with the scale of a key. Think about pitches that may be the 7th degree of a scale (the leading note) or the 3rd (which will give a clue about major or minor tonality). Compare what you see on the page with what you hear in the recording.

2. Describe the tonality in the following places: bars 35–39; bars 43–46; bars 51–54.

3. Identify the chords used at the following points: bar 69^1; bar 71^1; bar 72^1; bar 73^1.

The end of the tutti exposition

After the contrasts of the first 76 bars, the exposition concludes with a strong theme (2c), reinforcing the tonic key with alternating tonic and dominant chords. The woodwind and brass have sustained chords, while the second violins and violas have repeated semiquavers to maintain the energy and intensity of the sound. The viola part has three notes: the direction of the note stems in the notation instructs one player on each desk to double stop the upper two notes, while the other player plays the lower note. A roll on the timpani supports the answering theme in the cellos and basses.

In preparing for the exam, remember that you are expected to be able to locate a passage in relation to the structure of the movement. Does the given passage come from the exposition, development or recapitulation? Is it at the beginning or end of these sections? Are you able to describe briefly the music that comes before this passage, or the music that follows?

Exercise 31

By the end of the exposition the main musical ideas have been stated for the first time; in the rest of the movement Beethoven repeats and varies this material. While the first subject material can appear in a different order from the exposition, the second subject material is presented in the same order (apart from in the Coda).

Complete the table below to show Beethoven's treatment of the second subject material.

FIVE STATEMENTS OF THE SECOND SUBJECT THEME

Location	Instrumentation	Tonality	What comes next
Bars 43–89 Tutti exposition	Orchestra No solo violin part	Tonic, D major 2b in tonic minor, D minor	First entry of solo violin Based on V^7 chord Leading to solo exposition
Bars 144–195			
Bars 239–284			
Bars 418–469			
Bars 511–535 Coda			The end of the movement

Exercise 32

Find the Italian terms in the score that have the following meanings, where both (woodwind) instruments play the printed part:

- ➢ sweetly

- ➢ expressively

- ➢ (strings) pizzicato, plucked

- ➢ a little crescendo, very gradually getting louder

- ➢ always soft

- ➢ sforzando, a strong accent

- ➢ suddenly loud, then quiet

- ➢ play on the D and G strings

- ➢ trill, rapidly alternate two neighbouring pitches.

Solo 1 (Solo Exposition)

Instead of closing the orchestral exposition with a perfect cadence at bar 88, Beethoven uses the unresolved dominant 7th chord (A^7) as the background for the entrance of the soloist. In bar 89, the soloist outlines the notes of the dominant 7th chord on an ascending arpeggio of octave leaps. In bar 91, the solo violin reaches a *sforzando* on a high G, the 7th note of the A major chord.

Bowing

The bowing is indicated by the slurs over the notes: long bows for the triplets; quicker changes of bow for the pairs of semiquavers; finally, detached bowing for the scale up to top D (bars 100–101), the highest note at the start of the solo. Control of the bow is an important part of the skills of the violinist. Different bow strokes are used to articulate the notes in a different way. More frequent changes of bow make it easier to project the sound. Beethoven's bowing marks are not always clear. For example longer phrase marks look like an instruction to use long bows. In listening to performances of the first movement you may notice players making their own changes to the bowing. If you do not play the violin you may find it useful to get a violinist to demonstrate how the bow can be used.

Violin solo

From bar 101 the solo exposition repeats themes from the beginning of the movement, with the orchestral parts largely unchanged. The solo violin adds an extra layer to the texture and provides more rhythmic movement:

- ➢ The opening theme is played in heterophony with the woodwind; the violin decorates the theme with a quaver/two semiquaver figure (bar 103[4] onwards) an octave higher than the woodwind melody

- ➢ Ascending arpeggios in triplets (bars 111 and 113), covering the full range of the violin; the emphasis on G and C♯ (a tritone apart) on each beat matches the dissonance of the strings

> ➢ Syncopated octave leaps decorate the descending minims in the violins (bars 114–115)

> ➢ Legato semiquavers (bars 116–117) elaborate the longer note values of the original.

At bar 122 Beethoven begins to change the order of ideas, reducing the role of the orchestra as the solo part begins to dominate. The dramatic *fortissimo* theme on the full orchestra (1d) goes; it will be used when the first solo is over at the beginning of the development. Even the grand closing theme of the exposition (1e, at bar 178) is now played softly, with the orchestra reduced to strings, oboes and bassoons.

The solo part becomes more varied and challenging, changing quickly from one type of figuration to the next. Look also at the relationship between the solo and the orchestra in the following passage described in the table below:

Bars	Thematic material	Orchestra	Violin solo
126–133	1c D minor	Strings	Elaboration of ascending scale theme, marked *dolce*: in rapid semiquaver octave leaps, then in appoggiaturas, then ascending scales with 'turn' ornaments; difficult to play in a very high register.
134–143	1e Modulating to the dominant key	Antiphony between woodwind and strings	Continuous semiquaver movement (variation of five-note semiquaver figure from bar 35). Ends on figuration around the E (dominant note of the new dominant key), augmentation of rhythmic values, leading to trill.
144–151	2a A major	Clarinets and bassoons in 3rds; pizzicato cellos basses	Trill on E, then plays the second phrase an octave higher.
152–165	2b Dominant minor, A minor	Melody in first violins and violas, with pizzicato chords	Triplet figures, octave leaps, wider leaps, descending countermelody against ascending phrases in the melody. Covers a wide range.
166–177	1b	Sustained strings; dominant pedal in oboes and clarinets	Elaboration of 'timpani motif' with chromatic triplets on final note. Virtuosic arpeggios begin at bar 172 – ascending slurred (in one bow), then detached with turns, then detached semiquavers ascending and descending.
178–194	2c	Strings, oboes and bassoons (clarinets later)	Scale and arpeggio figures in semiquavers.
195–224	New treatment of timpani motif	Homophonic strings; clarinets and bassoons play motif in harmony, sustained V^7 chord	Ascending triplet figures, ascending chromatic scale (two octaves). The melody ascends to high E, followed by sustained trills ascending chromatically to the dominant (E). Solo ends with rapid scales and crescendo to the final high A.

Development

The development begins with the dramatic entrance of the full orchestra on the interrupted cadence (which keeps the momentum of the music going) at bar 224. The 1d material is heard for the first time since bar 28. From this point the development continues as a repeat of the tutti exposition in the dominant key and as a repeat of the second subject. The direction *sempre* ***ff*** (always very loud) at bar 256 reminds the performers that the tutti needs to sound forceful. The constant movement of pairs of semiquavers in the second violins and violas helps to retain the intensity. Notice how the chromatic A♯ of the 1b motif (at bar 261) is repeated with an enharmonic change to B♭ (at bar 263), becoming the 7th of a dominant 7th chord in F major (C^7). The change in the bass from C♯ to C♮ (bar 264) leads to a modulation to the distant key of C major for the closing theme (1e).

The violin begins its second solo by returning to the same introduction material as before (compare bars 284–299 with bars 89–101) – however, this time it is in the new key of C major. At bar 300 the music unexpectedly moves to an F♯; there is a gap of four octaves between the violin and the cellos (which are playing the opening motif *pianissimo* with the double basses). The first subject returns in B minor over a dominant pedal.

The repetition of the rhythm of the 'timpani motif' (and the melodic version of it which develops from bar 307) is an important feature in the rest of the development section. The motif develops as follows:

> ➤ The bassoons play in 3rds at a crotchet pace, then at bar 315 in diminution (quavers)

> ➤ The strings play as repeated notes (bars 308, 310 and so on), answering the bassoons antiphonally

> ➤ The horns play in octaves on D for eight bars (beginning at bar 330), accompanying a new solo melody in G minor

> ➤ Bassoons take up the dominant pedal on B♭ , as the music moves into E♭ major (bars 338–344)

> ➤ Trumpets and timpani play an A pedal (bars 346–357) in D minor, breaking into continuous repeated crotchets.

When a melody is augmented it is stretched out in longer note values. When it is diminished the opposite happens: the melody is presented in shorter note values.

There are long expressive melodic lines in the violin, with sighing suspensions at the ends of phrases. Sustained strings and the rocking movement of the quavers in the first violins provide the perfect accompaniment for the lyrical solo against the soft repetition of the motif in the wind instruments and timpani.

Recapitulation

When it was first heard at the beginning of the movement, the first subject theme was played softly in the woodwind; now at its return in the tonic key it is repeated with the force of the full orchestra. Once the fourth solo begins – the solo exposition – the role of the orchestra is reduced. The closing theme (from bar 452) is played quietly so that the violin can play its virtuoso semiquaver passagework. The recapitulation ends with a reprise of the long trills and scales which ended the exposition, followed again by the full orchestra with its sudden B♭ chord (bar 497). The music moves to a fermata (or pause) on a Ic chord (bar 510); this halt on an inconclusive chord is by convention the signal for the soloist's cadenza.

Cadenza

Soloists in the 18th century were expected to be able to improvise. A cadenza draws on themes from the movement, combined with the soloist's own elaborations and ideas. It had to sound as if it were made up on the spot. A trill on the penultimate note was the signal for the orchestra to restart and bring the movement to a close.

In practice, for safety, many soloists wrote out their cadenzas beforehand. Beethoven wrote cadenzas for the piano version of the violin solo (Op. 61a), which some violinists have adapted. There are many published cadenzas for this concerto (there are cadenzas in both the other two movements as well).

The quiet beginning of the coda (the term coda means the 'tail' of the movement, a closing section added to the usual structure) usually leads performers to end their cadenza softly.

Coda

At bar 511, the violin solo continues with the second subject theme, played on the G and D strings. It would be easier to play most of these notes on the D and A strings, but Beethoven instructs the soloist to play the notes higher up the fingerboard in order to exploit the richer, darker tone of the lower strings. The movement ends with the tutti closing theme from the second subject group (2c).

Further reading

Beethoven: Violin Concerto by Robin Stowell (*Cambridge Music Handbooks*). Cambridge University Press, 1998, ISBN 978-0-52-145159-8.

Exercise 33

1. The term 'virtuoso' is sometimes used to describe either players of exceptional accomplishment or music that is particularly difficult. What are the virtuoso characteristics of the violin solo in the first movement of Beethoven's D major concerto?

2. Listen to performances of the work by different violinists. Note any differences you hear in their interpretations. Consider differences and similarities in tempo, phrasing, dynamics, size of the orchestra, recorded balance between the solo and accompaniment, bowing, execution of ornaments, tone and vibrato.

Jazz recordings

Instrumental jazz, 1920–1960

At the beginning of the 1920s jazz was beginning to establish itself as a distinctive style of music. Musicians from New Orleans, the birthplace of jazz, were being drawn to the big cities of America, especially New York and Chicago, and the new technologies of recording and radio broadcasting were beginning to spread the sound of jazz throughout the United States and all over the world.

By 1960, the era in which jazz had often dominated popular music was over. There had been many rapid changes in the intervening 40 years – new musical styles had travelled far and caught on quickly. Compare this with the slower development of musical ideas in the 18th and 19th centuries, when Vivaldi, Haydn and Beethoven were composing.

Although jazz changed rapidly, you should not assume that later styles were better than earlier ones. Although we tend to talk of music 'developing', this means only that one style tended to grow out of another in sequence. There's no reason to suppose that Miles Davis is 'better' than Louis Armstrong or Jelly Roll Morton simply because he was working 30 years later. All of the jazz musicians you will be studying were among the best of their day, working with the styles and techniques of the time.

This is not the same as saying that jazz itself was over by 1960! Jazz standards continue to be played and new jazz performers continue to develop their styles.

Listening to the jazz recordings

Try to get copies of the specified recordings for each of the three works you will be studying (see the list on page 70). Take your time to get to know each work well. Jazz can seem confusing when you first hear it, but repeated listening will help you to make sense of the music. Discussing what you hear with others and working through the sections in this book will also help you.

In the exam you will only have an extract from the recording to work from. There will be no score to follow. In this book the structure of each work is laid out in a table, with the timing in minutes and seconds. There are also some musical examples, which are transcribed from the recordings.

The transcriptions are only a guide. Jazz scores are not as reliable as classical scores as it is impossible to notate all of the nuances of pitch and rhythm heard in jazz. Many jazz composers use only outline instrumental parts and communicate many of their ideas verbally. Improvised sections in your set works were not written down. You will need to listen carefully to hear how the recorded performance differs from what is written. The tables and examples are there to help you to get to know the work better.

Once you know your way around the work, put the examples and timings aside. Getting to know the work by ear is vital.

Key features of jazz

Frontline. These are the instruments that play the melody line. New Orleans jazz of the 1920s used trumpet, clarinet and trombone. The saxophone overtook the clarinet in popularity in the 1930s.

Rhythm section. This usually consists of drums, piano, banjo (or guitar in later jazz) and bass. The bass was usually a double bass played pizzicato (plucked) although the more powerful sound of a tuba was often used on early recordings. Sometimes the left hand of the pianist provides the bass. Chords are played by the piano and banjo or guitar. Players would often fill out the harmonies by adding extra notes, fills and syncopated rhythms – a technique called comping (an abbreviation of 'accompanying').

The bass in the earliest jazz tended to be in two-beat rhythm, reflecting its ragtime and march origins. The fourbeat pattern developed with the rise of the double bass as the main bass instrument.

Walking bass. A bass part, usually improvised, of four steady crotchets per bar, in which chord notes are often linked by passing notes to produce mainly stepwise movement. Earlier examples, from the late 1930s, are often quite simple but by the 1950s bass players were getting more adventurous in exploring the different registers of the instrument, giving their bass lines a character that matched the changing moods of the music as a whole.

Improvisation. The ability to make up and vary passages while performing, rather than reading them note by note from a copy, is an essential skill for a jazz musician. Improvisation often involves some degree of preparation of basic ideas and, in jazz, is usually based on an underlying chord pattern.

Arrangement. Not all jazz is improvised. Most of the works you are studying have an element of pre-composition. A jazz musician would need to be able to read music to make a living playing in the clubs and theatres of New York or Chicago. Written arrangements helped to improve standards of ensemble in the bigger bands.

Swing. Jazz is well known for its exciting rhythms. Early jazz reflected the syncopations of ragtime. In the 1920s, jazz musicians started replacing pairs of even quavers (known as **straight eights**) with a more lilting style in which the first quaver of each pair is held longer than the second. In addition, notes would often be anticipated or delayed in relation to the strictly maintained beat of the rhythm section. Swing is difficult to define or notate, and not everyone will agree whether a performance is swung or not.

Basing variations on a repeating chord structure is a composing technique that has been used for centuries. In jazz, the practice of borrowing just the chords of a standard, without the tune, developed originally as a way to avoid infringing the copyright of the popular song being used.

Changes. Many jazz pieces are based on a repeating chord pattern known as the changes. Each repetition of the chord progression is known as a **chorus**. One of the best-known changes is the chord pattern of the 12-bar blues. Others are often based on the harmonies of well-known popular songs of the time, known as **standards**, many of which are in 32-bar song form (AABA).

Blue notes and inflections. Listen out for small alterations in the pitch of notes. The most common are blue notes, involving a slight flattening of the 3rd, 5th or 7th degree of the scale. A keyboard instrument gives a poor impression of how these should sound. Listen to a jazz wind player or singer and see if you can hear the pitch of certain notes being pushed higher or lower for expressive effect. The pitch can also be bent while a note is being played.

Tone quality. Jazz musicians use many ways to vary the sound of their instruments, including different types of attack, production (such as deliberately rough or breathy tone), and vibrato (early jazz players used a fast vibrato, but the later works you are studying have slower vibrato). Mutes are often used to change the sound of brass instruments. Originally a mute could be a piece of cloth, a hat or any item which came to hand. The most common mutes today are the straight, cup, Harmon and plunger.

Double time. Playing in semiquavers instead of the usual quavers.

Recording technology

By 1920 the gramophone record had become the main way of bringing music to a wider audience, although it was soon to be joined by the newly developing medium of radio broadcasting. Recording companies spurred on the development of jazz by competing to search out new music and find artists who would be commercially successful.

Recording for the gramophone was originally an acoustic process, involving the use of a large recording horn that would capture the vibrations of the sound and record them as patterns on a wax disc. This would then be used to produce a mould from which multiple copies could be stamped onto brittle discs made from a naturally occuring compound called shellac. A shellac record was limited to three minutes of music on each side, which forced musicians to organise their pieces more compactly than they would in a live situation.

These early acoustic recordings suffered from problems of musical balance. The soloist(s) had to be placed close to the recording horn to be heard, and drums and bass instruments were difficult to record adequately – hence the reason why a tuba often replaced the double bass in the early years of recording.

Following the development of the first microphones suitable for music, electrical recording rapidly replaced the older acoustic method after 1925. The earliest works you are studying benefitted from this new process, although the end product was still a shellac disc with limited play time. Microphones improved in quality, and were soon able to cope with the bigger bands of the 1930s.

The development of tape recording and the LP (long-playing) record in the late 1940s revolutionised the record industry. Each side of an LP record offered at least 20 minutes of uninterrupted playing time, allowing jazz musicians to develop their ideas over a much longer period. Tape recording was equally revolutionary, since it became possible to edit and splice together sections recorded at different times, rather than always having to capture a complete performance in a single take. Furthermore, sound engineers could exercise better control of recording conditions, placing individual microphones in different positions so that the performance could be artificially balanced. This allowed instrumental combinations which would not be practical in a live situation. The work of the sound engineer also became increasingly important with the advent of stereo recording in the 1950s, towards the end of our period.

Securing a recording contract became an increasingly important part of the business of making jazz. Record sales generated larger audiences to hear live performances, which in turn offered the chance to secure bigger contracts with other companies later.

Further reading

Jazz by Mervyn Cooke. Thames and Hudson, 1998, ISBN 978-0-500203-18-7. A short, attractively presented guide to the history of jazz.

Jazz Styles: History and Analysis by Mark C. Gridley. Prentice Hall, 1978/2008, ISBN 978-0-136005-89-6. A detailed introduction to jazz for American college students. CDs are available separately to accompany the latest edition.

What to listen for in Jazz by Barry Kernfeld. Yale University Press, 1995, ISBN 978-0-300059-02-1. Looks at musical elements of jazz, with a range of examples on an accompanying CD.

A New History of Jazz by Alyn Shipton. Continuum, 1988/2007, ISBN 978-0-826417-89-3. An excellent and readable history.

Louis Armstrong: *Alligator Crawl*

This is one of the three jazz recordings set for exams in June 2011, January 2012, June 2012 and January 2013.

If you are sitting the exam in June 2013 or later, turn to the section starting on page 129.

Turn to page 149 for notes about exam questions on the jazz recordings.

Louis Armstrong (1901–1971) grew up in New Orleans, the city closely associated with the early development of jazz. Despite a deprived and troubled childhood, his talent for the cornet led to employment in dance-hall and riverboat bands, playing alongside some of the greatest jazz musicians of the day. These included cornet player Joe 'King' Oliver, who became a lasting influence. Oliver moved to Chicago, where opportunities to make a living from jazz were greater, and invited Armstrong to join his band there in 1922. After two years Armstrong moved to New York, recording with Bessie Smith and other early blues singers, and playing in the prestigious Fletcher Henderson Orchestra.

Armstrong's abilities as a soloist became widely known through recordings and radio broadcasts, and his swinging rhythm and highly melodic style were much admired and imitated. Gradually all band leaders, not just those for whom Armstrong worked, began to leave space in their arrangements for longer solos, accompanied by a reduced band or just the rhythm section.

The Hot Five and the Hot Seven

Armstrong's wife Lil Hardin, herself a pianist and band leader, encouraged Armstrong to return to Chicago. She was keen to promote his career, and collaborated with him in composing and arranging pieces for the Hot Five, a small band set up for a series of commercial recordings with the OKeh company in 1925–1928 with Louis Armstrong as the leader.

Initially Lil Hardin played the piano, but by the end of the series Louis had left her. Some of the best players were recruited to take part in the recordings, including Kid Ory (trombone), Johnny St Cyr (banjo), Johnny Dodds (clarinet) and his brother Warren 'Baby' Dodds (drums). Like Armstrong, they were all born in New Orleans and had joined the exodus to Chicago to work with King Oliver.

The line-up changed a few times, and the Hot Five expanded and became the Hot Seven. Armstrong's solos were very popular – a collection of them was printed for other cornet and trumpet players to learn – and they played a larger role as the series of recordings went on. His playing influenced not just trumpeters but other soloists as well. It helped make the New Orleans style well known and provided the basis for the development of jazz in the 1930s.

There are a number of factors which account for Louis Armstrong's success. He was an outstanding improviser: his melodies were bold and dramatic, yet seemed to unfold completely naturally. He had a strong, rich tone, an enormous range, and virtuosic technique.

Louis Armstrong was also regarded as much more of a 'hot' player than most of his contemporaries – he swung the rhythm much more than those who tended to rely on the genteel type of syncopation used in ragtime – and he was much more flexible in his use of rubato, constantly delaying or anticipating beats. Armstrong was also an influential jazz singer, particularly in his innovative use of the voice to imitate instrumental solos, improvising vocally to nonsense syllables in the style known as 'scat' singing.

Structure

The outer sections of *Alligator Crawl* are based on four choruses of a 12-bar blues in F major. This was one of the most common sets of changes in jazz at the time. The precise chords used in a classic blues do vary, but almost all include the following features:

➤ Three phrases of four-bars

➤ Chord I at the start of the first phrase and chord IV at the start of the second phrase (Bb in the key of F major)

➤ A slow harmonic pace (no more than one chord per bar – often the same chord will continue for two or even four bars).

The basic blues progression used by Armstrong is as follows, but in each chorus different chromatic and diminished harmonies are used to pass from one chord to the next:

> *Alligator Crawl*, recorded 10 May 1927 in Chicago for OKeh Records by Louis Armstrong and His Hot Seven.
>
> | | |
> |---|---|
> | Trumpet: | Louis Armstrong |
> | Trombone: | John Thomas |
> | Clarinet: | Johnny Dodds |
> | Piano: | Lil Hardin |
> | Banjo/guitar: | Johnny St Cyr |
> | Bass (tuba): | Pete Briggs |
> | Drums: | Warren 'Baby' Dodds |

The middle section, an extended solo by Armstrong, is based on *Alligator Crawl* by the jazz pianist, Fats Waller. It is a **paraphrase improvisation**, in which the notes of the original are outlined clearly at the start. As the solo progresses Armstrong adds his own improvisational detail. Here is the structure of the entire track:

> Fats Waller's own 1934 recording of *Alligator Crawl* can be heard at www.redhotjazz.com/Fats.html.

F major	Introduction	2 bars	0'00"	Trumpet
	Chorus 1	12 bars	0'04"	Clarinet
	Chorus 2	12 bars	0'32"	Ensemble
	Link	4 bars	1'00"	

C major	Solo A
	        B
	        A¹
		8 bars
		8 bars
		8+1 bars
			1'09"	Trumpet

F major	Chorus 3	12 bars	2'07"	Guitar
	Chorus 4	12 bars	2'32"	Ensemble

The brief unaccompanied introduction is played by Armstrong, beginning and ending on the dominant, C.

**Introduction
(trumpet)**

Although the 12-bar blues is based on primary triads (I, IV and V), these chords are not used in the type of functional, key-defining way found in the Baroque and Classical scores you have studied. This is largely the result of adding **blue notes** – particularly the flattened third and seventh degrees of the scale. Both are present

**Chorus 1
(clarinet)**

in the opening bars, despite the F-major tonality – the blue 3rd (A♭) in the clarinet solo and the blue 7th (E♭) in the harmony – and Johnny Dodds makes prominent use of high E♭s in bars 7–8:

> A smear is a slide up to a note from below, the fall off is a slide down at the end of a note, and a scoop is a slide down and back up again during the course of a note.

Notation cannot show every nuance of Dodds' highly expressive style, which includes glissandi, **smears**, **fall offs** and **scoops** to bend the pitch of many of the notes. He employs a fast, intense vibrato, that is typical of jazz clarinettists of the 1920s. The use of an arpeggio to move rapidly from high to low registers (the sextuplets in bar 10) is a very characteristic clarinet sound.

The piano and banjo keep time by **comping** in crotchets. The tuba plays the bass part, using a two-beat pattern with some faster rhythms to link the phrases. The trombone has low held notes. This style of accompaniment is used for most of the piece.

Chorus 2 (ensemble)

The second chorus features a style of **collective improvisation** known as **New Orleans polyphony**. Above a supportive chordal accompaniment and bass, each frontline instrument has its own melodic line and distinctive role:

➢ The trumpet has the melody, which here is in a high register and can be clearly heard above other parts in the recording.

➢ The clarinet has an elaborate countermelody, with rests at the beginning of phrases so that it answers the trumpet. Features of the clarinet solo from Chorus 1 reappear here: the melody from bar 3 is freely inverted and in bar 10 the clarinet has a held note followed by another rapidly descending arpeggio.

➢ The trombone has the tenor part in the texture, starting in minims and using glissandi and a pronounced vibrato.

Four bars link this section to the next, their purpose being to modulate to the dominant key of C major for Armstrong's solo in the central section of the work. They do this by emphasising the dominant of the new key. A pedal G is sounded throughout the four bars, over which a diminished 7th chord resolves to G^7. The octave leaps on G in the trombone add to the effect.

Central section: trumpet solo (with rhythm section)

New Orleans jazz tended to favour collective improvisation and short solos. In contrast, Louis Armstrong's trumpet solo here is unusually long and reflects not only the growing importance of the soloist in jazz at this time but also his status as band leader.

The solo is in three eight-bar sections, forming an ABA[1] structure, the last bar of which overlaps with the first bar of a two-bar link. The A sections are in C major, with a modulation to the dominant (G major) by the end of the first four bars. The B section is in E minor for the first four bars, and G major for the second:

In the first A section the solo stays in quite a narrow range – only an octave for most of its eight bars. Ends of phrases are either cut short with a staccato note or rounded off with vibrato on the final note. Notice the varied approach to the four-note chromatic figure in bar 1, when it is repeated later:

➤ Bar 1: quavers, with a syncopation and a repeated E

➤ Bar 5: semiquaver–quaver rhythm, then twice in semiquavers with the accent displaced

➤ Bar 17 (where the A section returns): quavers in a higher octave, then twice in semiquavers, varied and split between octaves.

The B section, starting in the contrasting key of E minor, consists of short one-bar phrases. Armstrong ends the first four bars with a blues inflection on a held G, with vibrato added at the end of the note (**terminal vibrato**). The subsequent return to G major, with the trumpet moving to a higher register, builds up to a long high A immediately before the return of the A section.

In the varied repeat of the A section, Armstrong's playing is more obviously virtuosic and dramatic, covering a range of two octaves and including several wide leaps (a 10th and a major 7th in bar 17, and an 11th in bar 19). Even so, he still makes the phrases sound melodic and unfold naturally. For example, in bars 18^4–20^2 the phrase covers a 12th but comes to a rest on a mid-range G.

Armstrong extends A^1 to nine bars in order to create a short link into the final section. Notice how he approaches the top A in bar 24 with a **rip** (a rapid slide up through the harmonic series) and then ends on a repeated tonic C in bar 25. This note is also the dominant of F major, thus preparing for the return of the blues choruses in the home key.

Chorus 3 (guitar) The contrast in texture between Johnny St Cyr's unaccompanied guitar solo and the band style of the rest of the piece disguises the return of the blues chorus at this point. He uses gently strummed chords decorated with some rhythmic movement, as well as both auxiliary notes and chromatic passing notes. The speed gradually gets faster as the solo progresses. Since no other instruments are playing, St Cyr is able to vary some of the harmonies in this chorus:

| F^7 |B♭ B♭m | F^7 C^7 |F^7 ‖B♭ |B♭m |F^7 C^7 |F F♯dim ‖ C^7 | C^7 |F^7 B♭–B♭m |C^7 ‖

Chorus 4 (ensemble) The final chorus returns to the style of collective improvisation used in Chorus 2, but at a slightly faster tempo. There are more high notes this time, with a wide, wailing vibrato from both trumpet and clarinet. Note the interplay between the frontline instruments.

At times the clarinet and trumpet move together, for example in the swing rhythms at the end of the chorus. When the trumpet briefly breaks into **double time** for an elaborate fill at the end of a phrase, the clarinet follows a bar later. Elsewhere one instrument is rhythmically active while the other has long notes or rests. The trombone has long notes in its tenor range, with glissandi and vibrato less prominent than they were in Chorus 2.

The comping style of the piano continues, but the softer guitar chords do not cut through the texture as effectively as the banjo.

There is no coda: the piece ends with a stroke on a suspended cymbal, with the player using his hand to stop the note.

Further listening

Try to listen to other recordings by Louis Armstrong and the Hot Five, for example *West End Blues* or *Hotter Than That*.

Exercise 34

1. Which features of Louis Armstrong's playing help account for his fame as a jazz musician?

2. Name the American city from which many of the members of Louis Armstrong's Hot Five came, and explain the importance of that city in the history of jazz.

3. Why do you think that Armstrong chose to use a tuba for the bass part in *Alligator Crawl*, rather than the more usual double bass?

4. Explain the meaning of each of the following terms:
   (i) comping   (ii) smear   (iii) rip   (iv) collective improvisation.

5. Which two degrees of the scale are most likely to be altered when playing blue notes?

Charlie Parker: *Ko-Ko*

Charlie Parker (1920–1955) was born in Kansas City in the USA. He taught himself the alto saxophone while at school, but initially didn't show any particular talent for the instrument. However, he practised intensely and modelled much of his playing on the style of Lester Young, who played in Count Basie's band in Kansas City. Increasing skill and confidence led to work with various bands and then a move to New York in 1939, although it was not until 1940 that his playing started to attract attention and he was able to work as a full-time professional.

Parker was particularly interested in developing the chordal basis of his improvisation. Like Dizzy Gillespie and other musicians in New York he was interested in expanding the possibilities of jazz through exploring new scales or taking ideas from contemporary classical music. He practised arpeggios, exploring new ways of using added notes, and developed a facility to play a tune in any key required.

When Parker was improvising he astonished other musicians with the pace and resourcefulness of his playing. Like Louis Armstrong before him, his virtuosity set a new standard for soloists which young players were eager to listen to and copy. His fast, aggressive style of jazz was a striking contrast to the accessible melodic style of the big bands. It was known as **bebop**, rebop or simply bop.

This is one of the three jazz recordings set for exams in June 2011, January 2012, June 2012 and January 2013.

If you are sitting the exam in June 2013 or later, turn to the section starting on page 129.

Turn to page 149 for notes about exam questions on the jazz recordings.

Bebop

The big bands of the 1930s were starting to struggle in the early 1940s. The success of radio and records had made a serious impact on live performance and a series of retaliatory strikes by musicians simply cut them off from these new areas of employment. America's entry into World War II at the end of 1941 absorbed huge human and economic resources, and the war resulted in shortages of many materials, including shellac for making records.

As big bands got fewer in number, musicians turned to playing in smaller groups and bebop was the new style that emerged. It continued to feature traditional structures such as the 12-bar blues and 32-bar (AABA) song form, but its distinctive hallmarks were:

➢ Small groups of players

➢ Fast, virtuoso solos, chiefly on the trumpet or saxophone

➢ Rapid twists and turns in melodies that cover a wide range

➢ Extensive improvisation, with pre-arranged sections normally limited to the beginning and end

➢ Time kept by a walking bass and a regular beat or swing rhythm on the ride cymbal

➢ Irregular phrasing and unpredictable off-beat accents

➢ Dissonant interpretations of standard chord changes, exploring techniques such as flattened 5ths, chord substitutions, added notes, chromaticism and unusual scales.

The trumpeter Dizzy Gillespie and the pianist Thelonious Monk were the first to pioneer the new style in 1940, trying it out in small groups after hours. A year later they were joined by Charlie Parker. To some extent the fast, intense style of bebop appears to be a reaction against the big band style, but its chief musicians were also successful performers in big bands. Dizzy Gillespie continued to work with big bands throughout his career.

Audiences, then and now, found it difficult to grasp the dissonance and irregular phrasing of bebop, which seemed to contradict the regular song structures outlined by the rhythm section. It had a much more intellectual appeal than music of the swing era – it was music to listen to, appreciate and discuss, rather than music to accompany singing and dancing.

Bebop musicians tended to regard their work as separate from the commercial mainstream of white-dominated swing bands. The fact that bebop exalted improvisation above arrangement reinforced a developing African-American identity. Gillespie and Monk adopted a consciously intellectual appearance, including berets and goatee beards, and bebop-influenced music soon started to appear in the concert hall, particularly in the works of Leonard Bernstein.

Strikes in the American music industry in 1942–1943 mean that the early development of bebop went virtually unrecorded. *Ko-Ko* was therefore among the first examples of bebop to be recorded.

The chord changes from the song *Cherokee*, written in 1938 by the British band-leader Ray Noble, had long appealed to Charlie Parker and soon became a jazz standard used by many musicians. The melody (not used by Parker) is very simple, but it is supported by richly chromatic harmony, with many added 7ths, 9ths, 13ths and other added notes, that form the basis of the changes.

The song has an AABA structure – usually described as **32-bar song form**, although notated by Noble in 64 bars rather than 32. The most distinctive feature of *Cherokee* is its bridge (the B section) which, instead of starting in the expected key of F major, opens with a chord of $F\#^{13}$ and then wends its way back to F (and then on to B♭ as the A section returns) by means of a **circle of 5ths**. Here is a slightly simplified outline of the changes in the original song:

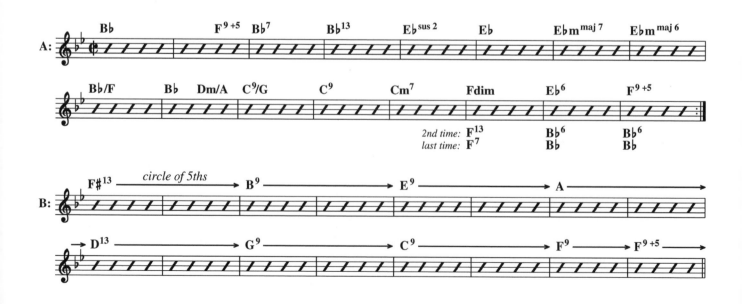

Structure

Ko-Ko starts with a 16-bar introduction, which is followed by two choruses of solo improvisation from Charlie Parker (based on the *Cherokee* changes). A drum break then leads to the return of the introduction (without its last few bars) to form a coda:

Introduction	32 bars	0'00"	Bars 1–8	Alto saxophone and trumpet in octaves	
		0'06"	Bars 9–16	Trumpet	
		0'12"	Bars 17–24	Alto saxophone	
		0'19"	Bars 25–32	Alto saxophone and trumpet in 3rds	
Chorus 1 (AABA)	64 bars	0'25"	Bars 1–16	A	
		0'38"	Bars 17–32	A	Alto saxophone solo
		0'51"	Bars 33–48	B	
		1'03"	Bars 49–64	A	
Chorus 2 (AABA)	64 bars	1'16"	Bars 1–16	A	
		1'29"	Bars 17–32	A	Alto saxophone solo
		1'42"	Bars 33–48	B	
		1'56"	Bars 49–64	A	
Drum solo	27 bars	2'07"			
Coda	28 bars	2'30"	Bars 1–8	Alto saxophone and trumpet in octaves	
		2'36"	Bars 9–16	Trumpet	
		2'43"	Bars 17–24	Alto saxophone	
		2'49"	Bars 25–28	Alto saxophone and trumpet in 3rds	

Rhythm section

Curly Russell is silent in the introduction, which is accompanied only by drums. During the choruses he plays a fast **walking bass** in crotchets, often using pairs of notes of the same pitch. In a style characteristic of bebop he makes frequent use of non-chord notes or added notes such as 9ths and 11ths, and often totally avoids the root notes of the harmony. Listen for passages in which he plays in the high register of the double bass.

Max Roach was one of the first to develop a new technique of drumming which went beyond its traditional time-keeping role. Although he uses the ride cymbal to articulate the crotchets of the walking bass, he uses the rest of the drum kit to develop some of the rhythmic ideas which he hears in the solos. He responds with unexpected bass drum or snare drum accents (sometimes known as 'bombs') on offbeats. The drumming is subtle, but it increases in activity to match the shape and intensity of the solo music.

A similar process is heard in the piano, played by Dizzy Gillespie. He accompanies Charlie Parker's solo with isolated chords, either staccato or sustained, to highlight changes in harmony – compare this with Lil Hardin's repeated chords which keep time in *Alligator Crawl*. Some chords are placed on strong beats, but more often he places mid- or high-register chords on weak beats. The left hand is used very little. The result is a light texture in the rhythm section.

Chords tend to be more dissonant than the lush original harmonies of *Cherokee* – for example, changing major intervals to minor or diminished ones. Gillespie also uses **chord substitutions**, meaning the replacement of a chord with a (usually more colourful) one that

Ko-Ko, recorded 26 November 1945 in New York for Savoy Records by Charlie Parker's Reboppers.

Alto saxophone: Charlie Parker
Trumpet/piano: Dizzy Gillespie
Bass: Curly Russell
Drums: Max Roach

Some mystery surrounds the piano part in *Ko-Ko*. Dizzy Gillespie had not expected to play trumpet in the work since Miles Davis was booked for the part. However, Davis left before *Ko-Ko* was recorded and so Gillespie played trumpet in the outer sections as well as piano in the choruses.

However, music had to be recorded in complete takes in those days, not in separate sections, and while the drum break gave Gillespie time to switch instrument for the ending, there is no similar gap after the introduction. It is therefore thought likely that a session pianist helped out in the first few bars of Charlie Parker's improvisation.

can serve a similar harmonic function. A favourite substitution was to replace a dominant chord with one that is a tritone away, as in the example left, where F⁷ in bar 1 is replaced by B⁹ at the same position in bar 2.

Commentary

Introduction

The introduction consists of four phrases of eight bars each and was probably written by Gillespie. He and Parker had a close working relationship, including practising each other's solos. This helped them to play fast, intricate bebop melodies accurately in unison or octaves – they choose octaves for the first eight bars.

Gillespie's trumpet solo in the next eight bars is in continuous quavers, but Parker follows this with an alto saxophone solo that divides his eight bars into three distinct phrases, a glimpse of the solo to come. Finally, both come together in 3rds for the final eight bars of the introduction.

The only accompaniment is from the drums, whose off-beat accents match those in the melody. The cymbal, double bass and piano are held back until the first chorus and the start of the changes.

Chorus 1
(Alto saxophone solo)

The first chorus is mostly diatonic, with occasional chromatic notes that mirror the changes in the chords, or as auxiliary or passing notes. The big-band jazz of the 1930s added 9ths, 11ths and 13ths to chords to enrich the harmony, but Parker was much more interested in using such added notes as important ingredients in his melody – the effect was to make his improvisations sound more dissonant than those of earlier jazz musicians.

If you listen carefully (the transcription printed opposite will help you follow it) you will notice that the solo is made up of different motifs – some are used more than once, often in varied form, and some can also be found in other recordings by Charlie Parker. He had a stock of hundreds of phrases and motifs which could be adapted at speed when improvising. The technique of weaving melodic formulae such as these into a continuous melodic line has been described as **formulaic improvisation**. In the hands of lesser players such a method could sound predictable, but Parker uses it to produce musical results and give his solo a natural sense of shape and development.

At the beginning, most of the phrases match the four-bar phrasing of *Cherokee*. Compare bars 17–20 with bars 1–4 and you will see that the first two A sections start with similar three-bar phrases, each followed by a bar's rest.

In the B section, the melody of bars 33–34 is repeated a tone lower in bars 37–38, but there are also examples of asymmetric phrasing. For instance, the phrase beginning in bar 47 continues into the first two bars of the final A section. Parker follows this with a four-bar phrase (bars 51–54) and then a six-bar phrase (bars 55–60).

Notice also how Charlie Parker often places accents on weak beats. The drums and piano contribute their own unexpected accents in response to his playing as well as filling in strong beats when the solo starts on an offbeat.

In the last four bars the quavers stop and a sustained dominant (F), echoed by the piano an octave lower, signals the end of the chorus. The drummer adds a syncopated rhythm on the bass drum in response (until now the bass drum has only been used for single accents or pairs of notes). Compare the way the band marks the end of this chorus and prepares for the next to the similar methods used by Louis Armstrong at the end of choruses in *Alligator Crawl*.

Charlie Parker begins his second chorus with a two-bar quotation from a well-known and challenging clarinet solo, *High Society*, a jazz display piece made famous by the New Orleans clarinettist Alphonse Picou. Here are the main features of this chorus:

**Chorus 2
(saxophone solo)**

		Solo	Accompaniment
A	1'16"	Quotation from *High Society* Mixed phrase lengths: 4+3+5+4 bars Moves rapidly across a two-octave range	Pizzicato walking bass, starting in high register Descending chromatic countermelody in piano
A	1'29"	Asymmetric phrasing continues: 2+6 bars	Piano chords are more regular
B	1'42"	Descending arpeggio figures 4+2 quavers create cross-rhythms Rapid descending scales in semiquavers	Modulations using circle of 5ths More active drum part
A	1'56"	Opening similar to A1 and A2 in Chorus 1	Bass in a higher register

Drum solo   Drum solos were unusual in early jazz and so the inclusion of one here is an indication that drummers were beginning to shake off their image of being simply time-keepers. The solo is faster than the rest of the piece and the drums are tuned higher than was usual, providing a brighter, more attacking tone for this solo.

Max Roach begins with clearly defined rhythmic patterns; by the end he is rapidly switching between the various parts of the drum kit while maintaining a constant rhythmic pattern. Listen to the variety in his playing, with its use of syncopation, figures that cut across the regular pulse and a range of timbres created by using both the centre and edge of the drum heads.

Coda   This final section is essentially a repeat of the introduction, without its last four bars, although notice the addition of cymbals. Parker's solo uses the same continuous quaver rhythm as Gillespie but whereas Gillespie's improvisation is scalic, Parker uses patterns of decorated, downwardly-spiralling arpeggios.

Exercise 35

1. Which features of *Ko-Ko* would you choose to show what is meant by bebop?

2. Make a table of the main features of Chorus 1, similar to the table printed above for Chorus 2. Then list the similarities and differences between the two choruses.

3. Explain what is meant by a chord substitution.

4. Compare the sounds and textures heard in *Ko-Ko* with those heard in *Alligator Crawl*.

5. What is the relevance of Ray Noble's song *Cherokee* to Charlie Parker's *Ko-Ko*?

Gil Evans/Miles Davis: *It Ain't Necessarily So*

This is one of the three jazz recordings set for exams in June 2011, January 2012, June 2012 and January 2013.

If you are sitting the exam in June 2013 or later, turn to the section starting on page 129.

Turn to page 149 for notes about exam questions on the jazz recordings.

Miles Davis (1926–1991) was one of the most influential jazz musicians in the second half of the 20th-century. He made rapid progress on the trumpet at school and at the age of 18 left for New York, where he was soon working with his musical idols, Charlie Parker and Dizzy Gillespie. He played most of the trumpet parts in Parker's recording sessions although, as mentioned earlier, Gillespie took over his role in *Ko-Ko*. Davis' own trumpet style was more economical than Gillespie's, less obviously bebop influenced. He preferred a middle-range sound, with a controlled use of vibrato, and a sensitive use of phrasing and silences.

In 1948, at the age of 22, Miles Davis formed his own band of nine players, working closely with the self-taught Canadian arranger, Gil Evans, who had arranged pieces for the Claude Thornhill band in New York. Thornhill's band was central in the development of a new style of **cool jazz**, employing instruments not previously used in jazz bands (such as the orchestral horn and tuba) to create striking new textures. Members of the band were encouraged to play without vibrato and the style was precise and considered, with a strong element of pre-composition in the arrangements – all of which greatly influenced Davis' own work.

In 1957 Miles Davis signed a recording contract with Columbia, who were keen to promote new styles of jazz. The result was three albums with Gil Evans as arranger, the second of which was *Porgy and Bess*. It consists of arrangements of 13 numbers from George Gershwin's popular opera *Porgy and Bess*, first staged in 1935. In the opera, *It Ain't Necessarily So* is sung by a cynical drug dealer named Sporting Life. The sinuously twisting main theme forms the basis of Evans' interpretation, and he retains the tempo and key of the original. However, he doesn't include the faster contrasting sections that occur in Gershwin's opera, although he does refer to their rising chromatic harmonies in his bridge sections (B1, B2 and B3 below).

Structure

A nine-bar introduction is followed by four choruses in 32-bar song form, the last of which has an AAAA phrase structure rather than the usual AABA:

B minor	Introduction	9 bars	0'00"	
G minor	Chorus 1	32 bars	0'35" 0'49" 1'03" 1'17"	A1 A2 B1 A3
	Chorus 2	32 bars	1'31" 1'45" 1'59" 2'14"	A4 A5 B2 A6
	Chorus 3	32 bars	2'28" 2'42" 2'55" 3'10"	A7 A8 B3 A9
	Chorus 4	32 bars	3'24" 3'38" 3'53" 4'07"	A10 A11 A12 A13

The 32-bar song form is interpreted very flexibly. For example, A7 at the start of Chorus 3 is a continuation of A6. The main melody returns in A9 and then continues into A10 at the start of the next chorus.

It Ain't Necessarily So from *Porgy and Bess* (by George Gershwin), recorded 29 July 1958 for Columbia Records in New York by Miles Davis and the Gil Evans Orchestra.

Five trumpets (soloist: Miles Davis)
Four trombones
Three orchestral horns
Tuba

Alto saxophone (Cannonball Adderley)
Flute / alto flute / clarinet (2 players)
Alto flute / bass clarinet (1 player)

Double bass (Paul Chambers)
Drums (Jimmy Cobb)

A riff is a short, repetitive pattern that can be adapted to different pitches to fit the current chord.

In a rimshot the drum head and the rim of the drum are hit simultaneously with the same stick, producing a strongly-accented note.

Dorian mode on G   Gm⁷

This table looks complicated because each eight-bar phrase has been labelled for reference later. It will be easier to remember the basic structure if you remember that it is similar to the repetitions of standard 32-bar song form used in *Ko-Ko* (but see left).

The band

The 19-piece band used for the recording was unusually large for jazz in the 1950s. It included Cannonball Adderley, Paul Chambers and Jimmy Cobb, who were to record the album *Kind of Blue* with Davis the following year.

The presence of only one saxophone in the line-up is surprising. Most big bands of the swing era in the 1930s had a large sax section. In contrast, Evans' band is dominated by the brass – 12 players in addition to the solo trumpet. The softer tone of the three horns – instruments more usually found in the symphony orchestra – is used to help blend the sound of the trumpets and trombones (similar to the way in which horns were often used to blend the different sounds of the woodwind section in a Classical orchestra). The tuba provides depth to the large brass section – the double bass would not be strong enough to provide this function by itself.

Some other orchestral instruments appear in the reed section, in which three of the four players are required to swap instruments for different pieces on the album. There are two alto flutes and a bass clarinet available for darker woodwind sounds in low registers where they do not cut across the solo line.

The rhythm section

The large orchestral sound means that a chord-playing instrument is not needed – rather in the way that a harpsichord was no longer necessary after orchestras increased in size during the Classical period.

The double bass and drums provide the backing for the long solo, supported by chordal **riffs** from horns and trombones. Chambers uses the four-beat walking bass style which was by now firmly established in jazz.

There is a steady swing rhythm on the ride cymbal and a **rimshot** on the fourth beat of most bars. Cobb uses some variety of tone and rhythm, but there is less sense of a musical commentary on the solo compared with Max Roach's drumming in *Ko-Ko*, where the small group encouraged more activity in the drum part.

Harmony

The harmonies in the A sections are based on a chord of Gm⁷ and use notes from the dorian mode on G, shown left. The original harmonies of the song also have a strongly modal feel – Gershwin alternated chords of G minor and C major in the main part of the accompaniment, although he also incorporated some chromatic harmonies. Davis had a strong interest in using modal scales in place of chord changes. He believed that set chord progressions limited the melodic possibilities of improvisation because players were more likely to depend on stock phrases they had used before. The musicians could be more inventive with their melodies if there were relatively few chord changes.

The B sections are more exciting in both texture and harmony, providing a clear contrast to the solo passages.

Commentary

The slow introduction contains a brief reference to another song from *Porgy and Bess – I Got Plenty of Nothin'* – which didn't receive an arrangement of its own on the album. This opening section is in the key of B minor, unrelated to the modal G minor of the rest of the track, and has a carefully calculated instrumentation:

Introduction

➤ Trumpet melody in a high register

➤ Low tremolo on D and F♯ in woodwind

➤ Trombone minims, descending chromatically

➤ Pizzicato triplets in double bass, forming a six-bar decorated tonic pedal

➤ Drums played with brushes.

In the last three bars, the solo melody ascends in step over chords of Bm⁷ and Am⁷. At the climax of the phrase a chromatic chord (D–F–A♭–C) substitutes for a dominant 7th in order to modulate to G minor for the rest of the piece.

The tempo for the main part of the track is twice the speed of the introduction. The drummer has changed to using sticks and the theme is introduced in **paraphrase** style, meaning that it outlines features of the original melody. Davis uses short motifs separated by silences, focusing on the descending perfect and diminished 5ths that are such a feature of the tune. Having only hinted at the melody in A1, Davis comes closer to quoting it in the first two phrases of A2:

Chorus 1 (A1 and A2)

Notice the use of **ghost notes** (marked with crossed noteheads) where the tone is almost inaudible. The horns play syncopated staccato triads in a riff of four chords (shown right) which forms the basis of the accompaniment for the rest of the piece. The accent on the last quaver of the bar, instead of the first, reinforces the swing feel of the music.

(B1) The band has a fuller part in all three B sections. Davis plays a descending scale, starting on the highest note heard in the introduction, and the accompaniment begins to ascend chromatically, with rich chords in brass and woodwind, and a steady crescendo throughout.

After four bars, as the solo trumpet drops out, the other trumpets add their brightness to the texture. The chords are in close harmony, the whole section moving in one rhythm. Notice how Gil Evans writes unexpected accents on weak beats to create syncopation. The crash cymbal is used to strengthen some of these accents and is also used at the end of the chorus.

(A3) The solo phrases are longer and more sustained in A3, with fewer silences. A new accompaniment motif in the trombones appears at the end of the chorus. The held chord (shown left) is underpinned by G in the bass so the A in the uppermost part forms a major 9th above the basic chord of Gm⁷, adding a richness to the harmony that is enhanced by the use of a type of vibrato produced by rapidly moving the trombone slide in and out.

Chorus 2 (A4 and A5) The motif printed above is repeated at the end of A4, but now with the held chord replaced by a syncopated rhythm. In A5, instead of exploring a restricted number of mid-range notes, Davis plays a three-note figure in a long descending sequence, followed by an ascending scale. The whole passage takes the melody from the highest range to the lowest and back again. The accompanying horn riff is changed rhythmically and then freely inverted towards the end of A5.

(B2) The chords are played in legato minims. A short chord, backed up by bass drum, creates a dramatic break in the middle of the ascending scale. As the chords continue to ascend, notice the bass moving in alternate descending 5ths and ascending 4ths. The complex harmonies build up to a final dissonant chord, taking full advantage of the number of instruments in the orchestra to create a very rich spacing of the chord.

(A6) Davis begins with the falling augmented 4th from bar 5 of A1. The texture has been reduced to trumpet and rhythm section plus quiet brass riffs. Miles Davis uses scale passages and references to the intervals of the melody. He regularly returns to G, D and D♭, for example at the beginning and end of phrases. The motifs in the brass accompaniment are fragmented, altered in shape and rhythmically displaced (shifted to start on unexpected beats). There is a feeling of uncertainty and exploration.

Chorus 3 (A7 and A8) The style of A6 continues into A7 at the start of this third chorus. In A8, the accompanying riff is used as expected in the first half, and then inverted in the second half. The diminuendo by the band reduces the accompaniment to pianissimo.

(B3) The dramatic return of the full band, playing in a triplet rhythm, shows Evans' skill as an arranger: chords in different sections of the band move in contrary motion with each other and then, after a four-beat silence, move together in the same direction. In the second half of this bridge, the soloist's ascending scale from B2 returns, along with the accompaniment in ascending minims. The latter is now scored for horns and trombones only, so that Miles Davis will not be hidden by the band trumpets – they simply enter for a single **stab chord** of G minor, with a high G as the top note.

The original melody returns, with the accompaniment of A1.

(A9)

In A10 Evans continues the sense of recapitulation by continuing with the original melody and now the accompaniment of A2. In A11 the horn riffs are varied, but soon revert to the original two bars just before A12. Remember that there is no bridge in this final chorus – the B section is replaced by another appearance of the A section, which we have called A12. The texture is thinner, with no heavy brass, the horns play quietly, and the dynamic reduces to pianissimo in the rhythm section at the end of A13. The soloist starts a final descending scale on a high D. This final section is based around a repeated A, which sounds unfinished, although the double bass has a final tonic G to end.

**Chorus 4
(A10, A11, A12
and A13)**

> **Further reading**
>
> *Miles Davis: The Definitive Biography* by Ian Carr. Harper Collins, 1982/1999, ISBN 978-0-006530-26-8. An absorbing account of Davis' life and music, including his later experiments with jazz-rock fusion.

Exercise 36

1. How does the trumpet style of Miles Davis differ from that of Dizzy Gillespie?

2. What impact did developments in studio technology have on the recording of *It Ain't Necessarily So?*

3. Explain the different roles played by George Gershwin, Gil Evans and Miles Davis in the creation of this version of *It Ain't Necessarily So.*

4. Explain each of the following terms:
   (i) riff   (ii) rimshot   (iii) ghost note   (iv) bridge.

Louis Armstrong: *Hotter Than That*

Trumpeter Louis Armstrong (1901–1971) is a key figure among the New Orleans musicians who pioneered jazz. Like many other musicians, he left New Orleans as a young man for the wider opportunities of the northern cities of the United States. Initially he went to play for his mentor King Oliver in Chicago. Until the depression of the 1930s Chicago rivalled New York for theatre and cabaret (most of these establishments were run by organised crime); there was plenty of work for talented jazz musicians.

Armstrong enjoyed a successful period in New York with the Fletcher Henderson Orchestra, attracting much attention as a soloist. In 1925 Armstrong's wife, Lil Hardin, brought him back to Chicago with the promise of a job in Bill Bottoms' Dreamland Café. He was paid $75 a week: an unusually large wage at the time for a black musician.

This is one of the three jazz recordings set for exams in June 2013, January 2014, June 2014 and January 2015.

Turn to page 149 for notes about exam questions on the jazz recordings.

For more information on Louis Armstrong and the Hot Five, see the introduction to *Alligator Crawl* (which he recorded earlier in the same year) on page 114.

As a band soloist at the Dreamland Café, Armstrong led a busy life. In the afternoon, for the black audiences at the Vendome Theatre, there would be an overture from the whole band, followed by music to accompany a silent movie. A solo spot would then follow in the interval: usually a jazz number, or sometimes an arrangement of an operatic aria. The evening Dreamland cabaret included music for a floor show and for dancing, usually standards or numbers from Broadway shows. Most of the work was accompanying, but Armstrong's solo improvisations attracted the admiration of many Chicago musicians.

Hot Five and Hot Seven recordings

For Lil Hardin, having her husband with her in Chicago meant that she was both promoting his career and preventing his womanising (which had been a problem for her while Armstrong had been away in New York). Together as musicians, Armstrong and Hardin worked on much of the material for the Hot Five recordings, produced for the OKeh Phonograph Corporation.

As the Hot Five and Hot Seven recordings progressed, Armstrong's solo role increased. His performance became the focus of the recordings and an important factor in their commercial success. The key features of his style which made an impact on audiences were:

➤ His skill and resourcefulness at improvising, combining both interesting melodic detail and a satisfying overall shape

➤ His use of swing and rhythmic displacement, using rubato and cross rhythms much more freely than other contemporaries

➤ His ability to colour individual notes with vibrato, shakes, rips and falls, which gave his playing tremendous energy

➤ His trumpet technique, which employed a powerful tone and wide range

➤ His bold, dramatic solos that dominated the ensemble and enhanced his role as a virtuoso soloist

➤ His scat singing (improvised vocal solos to nonsense words).

Armstrong's style Despite the popularity of their recordings, the Hot Five did not perform live. The players were selected from among the best of the New Orleans musicians working in Chicago. Like Armstrong they were steeped in the New Orleans style and had played in many of the same bands, including Fate Marable's Riverboat Band, Kid Ory's own band in New Orleans, and with King Oliver in Chicago. For *Hotter Than That* Armstrong added the blues guitarist Lonnie Johnson, who had won a talent competition with OKeh and was a staff musician with the company.

Armstrong had already been recording with a larger group, promoted as the Hot Seven. For this line-up of seven the rhythm section included a tuba and drums, which gave a stronger accompaniment to his solos. However, in *Hotter Than That* there is no percussion and the bass is divided between the trombone and the left hand octaves of the piano.

The main focus of the piece is on Armstrong as soloist and in his duets with Johnson (on blues guitar). There are substantial solos from Dodds and Ory. The New Orleans style of **collective improvisation** is confined to the introduction and the second half of the final chorus.

Structure

The composition of *Hotter Than That* is credited to Lil Hardin. However, her original melody is lost and we are left with the arrangement as heard in the recording. The 32-bar chord pattern for each chorus is based on part of *Tiger Rag*, a standard for New Orleans players. Only primary chords are used to begin with: E♭ major, B♭7 and A♭. Note in the following extract how infrequently the chords change: E♭ for six bars, followed by B♭7 for eight bars, then E♭ for eight bars. By contrast the harmonic rhythm of the last eight bars is much faster, with a change of chord every four beats to drive the music forward to the end of the chorus.

Hotter Than That, recorded 13 December 1927 in Chicago for OKeh by Louis Armstrong and his Hot Five.

Trumpet/vocal: Louis Armstrong

Trombone: Edward 'Kid' Ory

Clarinet: Johnny Dodds

Guitar: Lonnie Johnson

Piano: Lil Hardin

Banjo: Johnny St Cyr

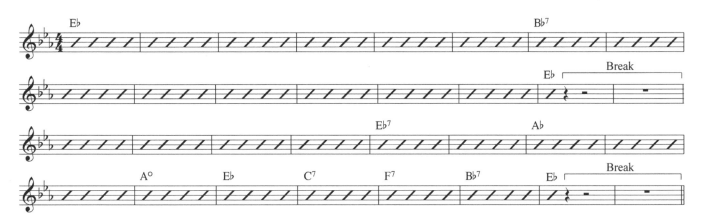

Each half of the chorus ends with a two-bar break, where the rhythm section stops dramatically for an unaccompanied solo. This becomes an important structural device. At the halfway point of a chorus it breaks up the solo effectively and creates a sudden change of texture; this offers an important point for the soloist to decorate between the two halves of his solo. Where the break occurs at the end of the chorus, the next musician can make a striking entrance before beginning their solo. The most effective use of the break is in the final chorus after the trombone solo, where Armstrong's ascending scale leads back to the final full ensemble.

Introduction	8 bars	0'00"	Ensemble – New Orleans style
Chorus 1	32 bars	0'09"	Trumpet solo (Louis Armstrong)
Chorus 2	32 bars	0'45"	Clarinet solo (Johnny Dodds)
Chorus 3	32 bars	1'21"	Vocal solo (Louis Armstrong)
Duet	16 bars	1'56"	Vocal + guitar (Lonnie Johnson) duet, no rhythm section
Link	4 bars	2'14"	Piano (Lil Hardin), a tempo
Chorus 4	16 bars	2'18"	Trombone solo (Kid Ory)
	16 bars	2'36"	Full ensemble – New Orleans style
Coda	4 bars	2'51"	Vocal + guitar duet

Introduction

New Orleans polyphony

The introduction makes use of the final eight bars of the chorus' 32-bar chord pattern. The texture is typical of New Orleans polyphony:

➤ The short phrases of the trumpet melody are heard clearly

➤ The agile clarinet countermelody is balanced much further back in the mix, but is more audible in its higher register or in the rests between the trumpet phrases

➤ The trombone begins in traditional tailgate style, with glissandi up to sustained semibreves, before breaking into crotchets at the end of the introduction.

Early jazz bands sometimes played on the back of a truck. The trombonist would be at the back (by the tailgate) so there was plenty of room to use the slide, especially when playing a glissando.

Chorus 1

The clarinet and trombone drop out, leaving the rhythm section to accompany the trumpet solo. Armstrong's solo is confident and well shaped. At the beginning of each of the first four phrases there is a two-note syncopated rhythm on the upbeat (see bars 0, 4, 8 and 12 in the example that follows). Armstrong's accent on the first note makes the syncopation a clear feature of the melody and gives it a strong sense of swing. The first full bar of each phrase is similar in rhythm (compare bars 1, 5, 9 and 13). The similarity of phrasing helps to make the improvisation highly melodic.

Trumpet

Most of the phrases extend over an octave, showing the soloist's agility and range. Note how the gradual ascent of the first notes of phrases contributes to energy in the melody: the solo begins on E♭ (bar 0 in the example), the second phrase on G (bar 4), the fourth phrase on A♭ (bar 12), and finally it reaches B♭ for the first note of the break. On the recording there is a 'rip' up to this B♭ note, which is like a very quick, subtle, glissando.

The second half of the solo breaks into a more varied and virtuosic pattern, with fewer rests between phrases; there are broken-chord figures and chromatic triplets. For the final phrase (bar 24) there is a sustained high G with a 'shake' (lip trill). This G anticipates the first note of the next phrase and provides an example of Armstrong's rhythmic freedom in his solos.

In the example the printed notation follows the jazz convention of writing swung quavers as even notes.

Chorus 2

The blues sound of Johnny Dodds' first note – which uses a clarinet 'smear' (jazz term for glissando) – makes a striking contrast with Armstrong. The solo begins in the high clarino (middle) and highest registers of the instrument. Dodds was known for his bright, assertive tone, which is even more piercing at these registers. The fast vibrato, which was fashionable in the 1920s, is most obvious at the end of long notes (known as 'terminal vibrato').

In the first few bars Dodds emphasises the strong crotchet beats of the bar, rather than using the syncopated upbeat of the trumpet solo. After a few bars he moves into swung quavers for the rest of the solo. The longer notes of the second break also make expressive use of a 'smear' (glissando) to add to the blues feel.

The accompaniment is in the banjo and piano only. Lil Hardin's energetic comping on the piano is not restricted to repeated chords. At the beginning of the chorus the bass octaves in the left hand are mostly alternating tonic and dominant, similar to the 'oom-pah' of the bass in a brass band. After a few bars the bass begins to move between registers. The right hands chords also move into a high register in places, which creates more variety in the texture.

Chorus 3

The break at the end of Chorus 2 introduces Armstrong's singing for the first time. The piano drops out of the accompaniment, which leaves the banjo comping and Lonnie Johnson improvising countermelodies on the guitar.

Scat The scat solos on some of the Hot Five recordings were very popular with the public. Armstrong is believed to have recalled that when he recorded *Heebie Jeebies* in 1926 he accidentally dropped the lyric sheet, forgot the words, and was forced to scat in order to complete the recording. Whatever the truth of this story, by the time of *Hotter Than That* in 1927 his scat choruses were a planned part of the composition. This technique was largely popularised by the Hot Five recordings.

Armstrong's vocal dexterity enables him to give the scat solos many of the same qualities as the earlier trumpet solo in Chorus 1. The first 16 bars have a similar overall shape, which includes the steady climb of the phrases moving towards the break. At this point Armstrong's glissando imitates a trumpet-style rip to a high B♭. Listen also for the regular use of smears, fall offs and vibrato. The use of smoother phrases in triplets exploits the melodic qualities of the singing voice, which contrast with the more instrumental rhythmic phrases used at the beginning of Chorus 3.

A smear is a slide up to a note from below, and a fall off is a slide down at the end of a note.

The second half is remarkable for its rhythmic organisation. Armstrong sings a succession of 24 dotted crotchets, which covers nine bars (see music example that follows). The polyrhythmic effect of dotted crotchets in the solo against the crotchet beat of the rhythm section creates a different pattern of syncopation in each bar. This was very unusual for its time and shows his gift for rhythmic freedom and invention.

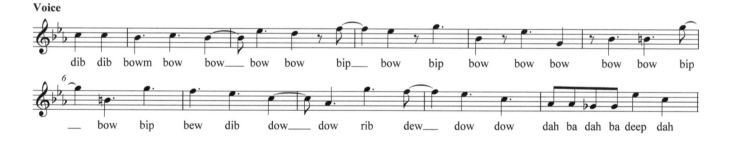

Duet

Armstrong himself takes the break at the end of his Chorus 3, which extends it to a phrase of four bars (instead of the standard two bars). The rhythm section remains silent as voice and guitar exchange two-bar phrases in call and response style. Armstrong and Johnson give a strong blues flavour to their dialogue. At the beginning of each phrase notice the variation of smears and microtonal inflections on the 3rd degree of the scale (G or G♭). The different tunings of G are made a feature of the dialogue; this tonal device exploits the expressive flexibility of blues tuning, compared to the western classical approach to intonation.

Chorus 4

After the interlude of the duet section, four bars of piano solo from Lil Hardin provide a **link** to the final chorus. Chorus 4 brings the music back to the original mood and tempo of the piece.

'Kid' Ory's trombone solo occupies the first half of the final chorus. He has four phrases of four bars each. Ory uses the slide on the trombone to decorate the pitches of the melody with three techniques: a glissando up to a note; a fall-off at the end of a note; a slide between notes. The rhythm section continues to drive forward an energetic accompaniment for the solo. In the background, Lil Hardin's piano decorates the harmony. Her style is typical of ragtime piano, with an elaborate countermelody in the right hand higher register.

The break at the end of the trombone solo brings Armstrong back to centre stage. Armstrong leads into the second half of Chorus 4 with an unaccompanied ascending scale in straight quavers, beginning as a chromatic scale and rising over an octave to a high B♭. The second half of the chorus begins in the **New Orleans polyphonic style**:

> See page 116 for more on the New Orleans style of collective improvisation in Armstrong's *Alligator Crawl.*

> The trumpet has repeated high B♭s in a syncopated rhythm for the first six bars, before breaking into the melody

> The clarinet plays an elaborate countermelody in a high register

> The trombone countermelody covers a wide range, providing some of the bass notes in the texture and some notes in the high register

> The rhythm section continues to comp.

The return of the full band at this point suggests a strong finale. Towards the end of Chorus 4 there is a dramatic sequence of 'stop time': the accompaniment plays short staccato chords separated by silences, which build up the anticipation for the end of the piece. The trumpet solo uses the syncopated dotted crotchet rhythms that had been used so effectively in the scat solo in Chorus 3.

In the closing bars of Chorus 4 Armstrong has one surprise left: he avoids the predictable full ensemble ending that the listener might expect. Instead Armstrong uses the final two-bar break at the end of Chorus 4 to return to the idea explored during the duet section: call and response with the guitar. The last guitar phrase reminds us of the blues style from the earlier dialogue. The final diminished chord makes for an intriguing and inconclusive ending.

Further reading

Early Jazz by Gunther Schuller. Oxford University Press, New York, 1968, ISBN 978-0-19-504043-0. Includes a significant chapter devoted to Louis Armstrong, with discussion and analysis of the structure of *Hotter Than That.*

Louis Armstrong: An American Genius by James Lincoln Collier. Oxford University Press, New York, 1985, ISBN 978-0-19-503727-2. A readable and informative biography, with much background information on the Hot Five period.

Exercise 37

1. Explain why Louis Armstrong made such an impact on audiences and musicians. Use examples from *Hotter Than That* to illustrate your answer.

2. Why do you think Armstrong added a guitar player to the line up of the Hot Five in this recording? What effect does it have?

3. How does the rhythm section of this piece differ from that of Duke Ellington in *Koko?*

4. What is meant by New Orleans style collective improvisation?

Duke Ellington: *Koko*

This is one of the three jazz recordings set for exams in June 2013, January 2014, June 2014 and January 2015.

Turn to page 149 for notes about exam questions on the jazz recordings.

Koko, recorded 6 March 1940 in Chicago for RCA Victor by Duke Ellington and His Famous Orchestra.

Alto saxophones: Johnny Hodges, Otto Hardwick

Clarinet: Barney Bigard

Tenor saxophone: Ben Webster

Baritone saxophone: Harry Carney

Trumpets: Wallace Jones, Cootie Williams, Rex Stewart

Trombones: Lawrence Brown, Joe 'Tricky Sam' Nanton, Juan Tizol

Guitar: Fred Guy

Piano: Duke Ellington

Double bass: Jimmy Blanton

Drums: Sonny Greer

Edward Kennedy 'Duke' Ellington (1899–1974) was brought up in Washington D.C. His musical middle-class parents arranged for him to be taught classical piano. However, the young Ellington preferred to learn the stride piano style of pianists such as James P. Johnson. With drummer Sonny Greer, Ellington formed his own band, the Washingtonians, and performed at the Kentucky Club in New York, toured dance venues and made his first recordings. It was at this time that he picked up the nickname 'Duke' – although some sources suggest that he acquired the name at an earlier time during his school years.

In the 1920s there was growing public demand for the new style of jazz known as swing. An important element in swing was the use of a much larger band (a big band or swing band) than in early jazz. The increase in size was because the music often accompanied dancing at venues of considerable size. The recording of *Koko* employs 15 players. The list of musicians for the *Koko* recording shows how the frontline soloists of New Orleans jazz had expanded into sections of trumpets, trombones and reeds (saxophones and clarinet).

Under the management of Irving Mills, Ellington's orchestra played in residency at the Cotton Club in Harlem between 1927 and 1931. The band performed for a wealthy white audience who enjoyed the vogue for exotic, African-style floorshows. Weekly radio broadcasts from the Cotton Club gave Ellington the type of public attention that few black bands had access to.

At the end of the Cotton Club residency Ellington's band toured Europe, where their music was already well known through their recordings. European critics were beginning to identify Ellington as the leading composer of jazz, comparing him favourably with classical composers. Returning to the United States the band toured extensively, and performed to both black and white audiences. Ellington composed many of his pieces while travelling on the train. Royalties from the sale of his songs made him one of the highest earning jazz musicians. Irving Mills' publicity encouraged the view of Ellington as an artist.

By 1940 Ellington's association with his manager Mills had ended; he had a new recording contract with the Victor label. Among the new musicians in the band were the saxophonist Ben Webster and a young bass player called Jimmy Blanton.

The Ellington effect Although solos were usually improvised, collective improvisation by the entire band was impractical with such large numbers, and so musical arrangements became essential in the swing era. These were often in the form of notated parts for the players. The size of the band allowed the leader or arranger to choose from a wide range of sounds and textures:

➢ Chords arranged for sections of reeds, trumpets or trombones, with one player to each note

➢ Unison melodies or riffs for a section

➢ Antiphonal effects of pitting one section against another, either as call and response or as countermelodies

> ➤ Solo improvisation with accompaniment from one or more contrasting sections (for example, a trumpet solo accompanied by reeds) and the rhythm section.

Ellington's compositions and arrangements were strongly influenced by the qualities of the individuals in the band. Not only solos but also individual parts in the ensemble were tailored to the tone and preferred playing style of the players. Many of the band's numbers were developed over time during rehearsal; ideas and suggestions would be incorporated before being written down definitively. In this way the Ellington band developed a sound and style that was very personal to Ellington and his players. Billy Strayhorn, Ellington's arranger, called it 'the Ellington effect'.

Many of Ellington's players stayed with his band for many years. Players like Johnny Hodges, Cootie Williams and Ben Webster became well known to the public through their solos on Ellington's recordings.

Jimmy Blanton's double-bass playing created an immediate effect on the Ellington orchestra. He was only in the band for a few years (1939–1941) before he died of tuberculosis at the age of 23. His round, well-projected tone and sense of swing can be heard in recordings of this time, including his duets with Duke Ellington (for example *Mr J. B. Blues*). Ellington gave Blanton solos to play and made sure that he was always well recorded. In the choruses of *Koko* Blanton uses the walking bass style, while Sonny Greer keeps time on the hi-hat and Fred Guy comps on guitar. Apart from his solo, Ellington's piano playing is used very sparingly; in most of the choruses it comprises single staccato chords to highlight the first note of the 'x' motif.

> Ellington recorded *Koko* again the following day after the 6 March recording. This alternative version is available on *Never No Lament: the Blanton-Webster Band* (RCA Bluebird 82876-50857-2), with interesting differences in the improvised solo parts.

The rhythm section

Structure

The piece is made up of an introduction, seven choruses in 12-bar blues form, and a coda. The key is E♭ minor (minor tonality is unusual for a blues) with the use of D♭s and C♭s, which give a feeling of the aeolian mode.

Introduction	8 bars	0'00"	
Chorus 1	12 bars	0'12"	Valve trombone solo (Juan Tizol)
Chorus 2	12 bars	0'32"	Trombone solo (Joe 'Tricky Sam' Nanton)
Chorus 3	12 bars	0'51"	
Chorus 4	12 bars	1'08"	Piano solo (Duke Ellington)
Chorus 5	12 bars	1'26"	3 trumpets in unison
Chorus 6	12 bars	1'44"	Double bass solo (Jimmy Blanton) + ensemble
Chorus 7	12 bars	2'03"	Full ensemble
Coda	12 bars	2'22"	

The 12-bar blues pattern follows a standard chord progression, albeit in a minor key:

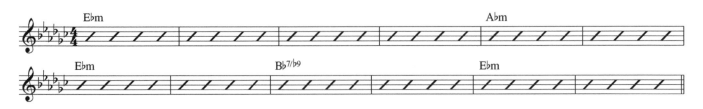

In *Koko* the music builds up gradually over the seven chorus repetitions of the blues. Ellington shows considerable control as he creates a sense of gathering momentum, using the four-note ostinato figure of the opening to create a sense of unity.

Introduction

The opening bars of *Koko* set the brooding, jungle mood from the outset. In addition to the minor key, the dark sound of the baritone saxophone plays a low tonic pedal on E♭. The brighter sounds of trumpets and higher reeds are not used in the introduction. The hollow sounds of the tom-tom and the crotchet beat of the bass drum add to the distinctive African colour of this passage. The four-note rhythm 'x' motif (as named by Ken Rattenbury, English jazz trumpeter and author on Duke Ellington) is stated here for the first time (see example that follows). The syncopated chords in the three trombones move in parallel, descending chromatically in each phrase.

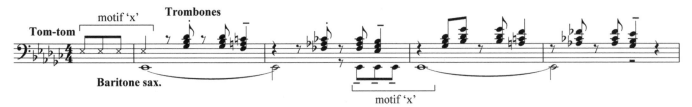

Chorus 1

Juan Tizol plays the opening melody on a valve trombone (shifts in position would make it impossible to manage smoothly on a slide trombone). The example that follows shows how the rhythm of the 'x' motif is used for the first four notes.

The trombone phrases are answered by close harmonies in the four saxophones, which move in parallel. In the example that follows, note the rich sounds of 7th chords and the bluesy sound of having D♭ and D♮ in the same chord (marked with an asterisk).

The double bass is playing a pizzicato walking bass, filling in the notes of the chords in stepwise motion. The drums have changed from the jungle colouring to keeping time on the hi-hat and bass drum.

The repeated two-bar phrasing between the trombone and saxophones is shortened in bars 9 and 10 to two one-bar phrases. At this point the piano adds a syncopated octave B♭ (a dominant pedal) with a crescendo, which adds momentum towards the next chorus.

Choruses 2 and 3

Joe Nanton has a double chorus for his trombone solo. His distinctive sound incorporates three effects. Firstly, he uses the growling 'ya-ya' sound for which he was well known. This sound is created using the plunger mute; it was common for all of Ellington's brass players. Secondly, Nanton uses a pixie (or straight) mute, which is fixed inside the trombone to create a buzz to the sound. Finally, his way of blowing contributed to the impression of words being pronounced. Nanton did his best to keep his methods secret in order to preserve his signature sound for himself.

Nanton's solo begins by emphasising the B♭, which Ellington had been repeating at the close of Chorus 1. He uses only a few pitches, but the vocalised sound with added smears and fall-offs creates a highly expressive calling effect that suits the jungle atmosphere of the piece. Nanton is accompanied by almost the full band:

1. The four saxophones (without clarinet) are playing in a two-bar riff in a low unison, using the 'x' motif and sustained notes. The same riff is used in both choruses. Single staccato chords on the piano mark the first note of the 'x' rhythm.

2. Three brass players (two trumpets and a trombone) play a syncopated rhythm, alternating repeated notes quickly between closed and open plunger mute positions. This is known as the 'du wah' effect because of the sound it makes. In notation the composer or arranger would write '+' over the note to indicate the mute and 'o' to create an open sound.

3. The rhythm section keeps time; it is led by Jimmy Blanton's very clearly recorded walking bass, with the guitar comping and the drums keeping time.

The second half of the solo (Chorus 3) begins with higher pitches: the plunger mute is tight against the bell of the instrument, which restricts the sound further. Nanton then returns to the ya-ya style of playing to conclude the end of his solo.

Chorus 4

For Duke Ellington's piano solo the accompanying riffs begin to move in one-bar phrases. The aeolian mode is reinforced by the repeated D♭s (the 7th of the E♭ minor chord) on each first beat.

The boldest harmony is in the dissonant piano solo. The right hand plays a whole-tone chord of F♭ – G♭ – B♭ – C, followed closely by a whole tone scale in semiquavers (ascending and descending over an octave and a half). The use of the bright high register of the piano emphasises its polytonal dissonance as it clashes with the E♭ minor chord in the rest of the band (and the left hand of the piano).

Four bars later, a whole-tone scale starting on C♭ (listen out for the F♮ and G♮ in the scale) creates a similar colourful dissonance against the A♭ minor chord. The solo ends with a syncopated E♭m⁷ chord. Ellington arranges this chord so that it leaps in pairs that are a 10th apart across the range of the instrument (for example, playing E♭ with a G♭ that is an octave and a 3rd higher).

Chorus 5

The riff moves to the trumpets for the first time in Chorus 5, and reverts back to two-bar phrases. The repeated phrase is higher so that the 9th of the chord is the most prominent; it is more dissonant than the 7th in the previous chorus.

The sound of the unison trumpets with plunger mutes half open gives the music a more insistent feel. Apart from the piano, the whole ensemble is playing for Chorus 5. The reeds and trombones play a two-note rhythm and sustained chords, which answer each other antiphonally. The clarinet takes the highest note in the chord. The baritone sax has its own decorated figure.

Chorus 6

The music in *Koko* has built up consistently so far. In Chorus 6, the 'x' motif is now harmonised by each section in turn. The example below shows how each section enters in imitation at a distance of one minim apart. The full band sustains the chord until an emphatic stop on two *fortissimo* repeated quavers.

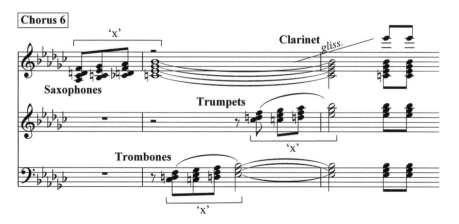

The double bass breaks the dramatic pause with a two-bar solo, which comprises a descending scale in walking bass crotchets. The rest of the chorus continues to alternate between the full band in imitation and solo bass in two-bar phrases. This type of chorus is often referred to as a 'chase chorus'.

Chorus 7

The full ensemble takes over for the final climactic chorus, known as a 'shout chorus'. The melody is in unison saxophones. The clarinet supplies the highest note of the sustained chords in the brass section. Note the highly dissonant chords in this chorus. The E♭ minor chord at the beginning now includes a 7th, 9th and an 11th. Note also the insistent E♮s in the saxophones in bar 9 of the example: this causes a dissonance of a tritone (augmented 4th) against the B♭ in the bass. The phrase also includes whole-tone inflections, which Ellington had referred to earlier in his piano solo.

Further reading

Duke Ellington, Jazz Composer by Ken Rattenbury. Yale University Press, 1990, ISBN 978-0-300055-07-8. Includes a detailed discussion of Ellington's style and a full score and analysis of *Koko*.

The Duke Ellington Reader edited by Mark Tucker. Oxford University Press, New York, 1993, ISBN 978-0-195093-91-9. A collection of writings about Duke Ellington, which comprise reviews and articles from his contemporaries. Also includes Richard Boyer's article *The Hot Bach* (1944), which gives a good insight into Ellington's life on the road and his reputation at the time in the United States and abroad.

This is one of the three jazz recordings set for exams in June 2013, January 2014, June 2014 and January 2015.

Turn to page 149 for notes about exam questions on the jazz recordings.

Coda

The coda concludes *Koko* with a return to material from the introduction. This time, however, the orchestration is reduced to baritone sax, trombones and rhythm section. The final bars bring the whole band in, section by section, in ascending phrases. At this point 'straight eights' replace the swung rhythm (which had been a characteristic of the piece) to bring the music to a close.

Exercise 38

1. What is meant by the jungle style?

2. Why do you think the big bands became popular in the 1930s and 1940s?

3. Explain the meaning of the following terms:

   a.   Walking bass

   b.   Shout chorus

   c.   Straight eights.

4. Describe how Ellington uses harmony and tonality in *Koko*.

5. Ellington's ability to create a sound that was unique to his band is often referred to as 'the Ellington Effect'. Give examples of how Ellington employs his signature sounds in this arrangement of *Koko*.

Miles Davis: *Boplicity*

Miles Davis (1926–1991) came to New York in 1944 as a teenager to study at the Julliard School of Music. He dropped out of college quickly to follow his idol Charlie Parker. By the age of 19 he was playing trumpet in Parker's quintet and making his first recordings.

The bebop style of Parker and trumpeter Dizzy Gillespie was fast and virtuosic. Although it was possible to dance to bebop, audiences tended not to. Bebop's hard-driven pace, dissonant harmonies and lack of easy melodies made it music for listening to rather than for dancing. Parker and his circle were happy to enjoy the intellectual status of being artists instead of entertainers. They discussed ideas about jazz music, such as how to construct new scales or chords. The group also took an interest in developments in classical music: Stravinsky, Ravel, Bartók and Prokofiev were favourite composers. The centre of much of these discussions was at the New York home of Canadian arranger Gil Evans.

By 1948 Miles Davis was breaking away from Parker and beginning to form his own groups. He was dissatisfied with bebop as a style. Davis avoided the fast-paced virtuosity that had been typical of Parker and Gillespie, and developed his own distinctive trumpet style:

➢ A quiet, understated sound, using the middle register, with very little vibrato

➢ Pitch bends at the beginning and ends of notes, and a wide variety of notes

➢ An economical style, avoiding double time and using silence

➢ A flexible sense of timing, anticipating and delaying notes against the underlying pulse.

Gil Evans

Gil Evans was the arranger for the Claude Thornhill band. At the end of World War II the big bands were struggling. Although the Ellington and Basie bands continued to be successful, the public appetite for big band swing was diminishing. Whereas bands had once toured the country between week-long engagements, now even Duke Ellington's band played mostly one-night stands. For the record companies, singers were likely to sell better than instrumental jazz.

Thornhill worked hard to keep his band going. He adapted classical pieces for the swing band idiom, and developed a distinctive sound that became the basis of Gil Evans' arranging style:

➢ Unusual instrumentation, including the use of French horn and tuba

➢ Minimal use of vibrato

➢ Emphasis on soft, subdued sounds in low registers.

Most swing bands used sections of brass and reeds as contrasting groups. The antiphonal effect of contrasting sounds was important in band arrangements, such as in Duke Ellington's *Koko* (see pages 136–141). But Ellington's virtuoso band was also noted for its subtle arrangements and unusual combinations of instrumental timbres; features that both Davis and Evans admired. Gil Evans' technique of arranging extended the Ellington approach. The soft vibrato-less tone in the Thornhill band allowed Evans to blend the sounds of instruments from different sections of the band, and to create richly textured chords and subtle effects of instrumental colour.

See pages 124–125 for more information on the Davis/Evans collaboration on their album *Porgy and Bess*.

Birth of the Cool

Boplicity was one of 12 tracks recorded by Miles Davis and his Nonet in three sessions for Capitol Records in 1949–50. The recordings were released in pairs: one on each side of a standard three-minute disc, playing at 78 rpm. When *Boplicity* was reissued in 1957 it was in LP (long playing) format, a single album of 11 tracks, playing at 33 rpm. For this release the album's title was *Birth of the Cool.*

The *Birth of the Cool* recordings grew out of the discussions and active collaboration of the group gathered around Gil Evans. Many of the musicians involved were arrangers themselves, notably Gerry Mulligan (who is credited with three numbers). *Boplicity* (also known as 'Be Bop Lives') is credited for business reasons to Davis' mother, Cleo Henry, but the melody and arrangement are by Davis and Evans.

The nonet formation – nine players, comprising six horns (wind/brass instruments) and the standard rhythm section of piano, bass and drums – was considered by the group to be the ideal. At a time when bands featured a large group of saxophones, it was unusual to have only two. The French horn is used to blend the sound of the brass and saxophones. The tuba adds depth to the ensemble. Tuba player Bill Barber from the Thornhill band played in all of the *Birth of the Cool* recordings (as did saxophonists Mulligan and Lee Konitz).

Miles Davis was very much the leader of the band. His understated, coolly expressive approach set the tone for the other soloists. He arranged the recording contract with Capitol and booked a few engagements. The band's fresh approach drew interest from musicians and critics, but the public remained largely indifferent.

By the 1957 release Miles Davis was an established and marketable star. During the early 1950s the trend towards a softer, less dauntingly complex style of jazz became known as 'cool jazz'. Some of the nonet's musicians were key figures in the development of this style, notably Lee Konitz, Gerry Mulligan and John Lewis. The rebranding of the recordings as *Birth of the Cool* was a recognition of the influence and importance of these sessions.

Boplicity, recorded 22 April 1949 in New York for Capitol Records by Miles Davis and His Orchestra.

Trumpet: Miles Davis

Trombones: J.J. Johnson

French horn: Sandy Siegelstein

Tuba: John 'Bill' Barber

Alto saxophone: Lee Konitz

Baritone saxophone: Gerry Mulligan

Piano: John Lewis

Double bass: Nelson Boyd

Drums: Kenny Clarke

Structure

Boplicity is based on a standard 32-bar song form. The moderate tempo meant that it could only be played three times within the three-minute limit of a 78 rpm disc.

Chorus 1	32 bars	0'00"	A (8 bars)	Full ensemble (no piano)
			A (8 bars)	
			B (8 bars)	
			A (8 bars)	
Chorus 2	34 bars	0'57"	A (8 bars)	Baritone saxophone solo (Gerry Mulligan)
			A (8 bars)	
		1'25"	B (6 bars)	Full ensemble (no piano)
			+4 bars	Trumpet solo (Miles Davis)
			A (8 bars)	Full ensemble (no piano)

Chorus 3	32 bars + 1 bar	1'57"	A (8 bars)	Trumpet solo with ensemble
			A (8 bars)	Trumpet solo with rhythm section
		2'25"	B (8 bars)	Piano solo (John Lewis)
			A (9 bars)	Full ensemble (no piano)

Despite the AABA form, *Boplicity* is not easy to follow when listening to the recording. A number of features disguise the shape of the choruses:

➢ The bridge in Chorus 2 is extended to ten bars (six bars of full ensemble followed by four bars of trumpet solo)

➢ The trumpet solo begins during the B section of Chorus 2 and then continues through to the next B section of Chorus 3; therefore, there is no change of soloist for the next chorus (Chorus 3)

➢ The consistent use of the frontline players to accompany the trumpet makes the start of Chorus 3 less obvious

➢ The accompaniment is fully written out, making the piece sound through-composed. Evans avoids the riff-based style that Ellington uses to mark his choruses

➢ The subtle harmonies of the opening A sections are not replicated in Choruses 2 and 3; each chorus has its own chord structure.

The rhythm section features the double bass playing a pizzicato walking bass. The drums are played with brushes throughout the piece. The piano is mostly silent during full ensemble passages, where the already richly scored textures do not need any additional chordal support from the piano.

Chorus 1

Boplicity has no introduction. The opening chorus is fully written out for the full ensemble, minus the piano. The melody on the trumpet is doubled an octave lower by the baritone saxophone. The six horns (wind/brass) form a rhythmic unit that plays complex chords in close harmony. The following example is the opening eight bars (section A) of Chorus 1.

The F major tonality is not immediately apparent. Evans begins with a Gm7 chord and uses chromatic chords; each F chord uses different extensions (7ths, 9ths, 11ths). Only in bars 6–7 does a dominant pedal of C suggest the key more clearly. Even the final chord has the rich sound of an 11th chord, with the G and B♭ sharpened to G♯ and B♮. (Try playing F major and E major triads at the same time to get the same effect.)

The first four bars are highly syncopated. The melody notes rarely coincide with the strong beat in double bass and drums. The triplet in bar 2 adds to the rhythmic flexibility of the melody. By contrast the answering phrase (bars 5–8) hits the strong beats regularly. There is a repeated ascending 3rd figure (marked 'b' in the Chorus 1 example) over the syncopated dominant pedal in the tuba and the clear offbeat hits of the cymbal. After the ambiguities of the opening, the second half of section A helps to provide the certainty of a completed phrase.

The B section has more conventional phrasing and chord progressions. The melody uses the six-note tag from the end of the trumpet's first phrase (bar 4, marked 'a' in the Chorus 1 example). The repetition of the 'a' motif gives this section a clear shape.

Chorus 2

Baritone sax solo The baritone saxophone is not a commonly used solo instrument. Gerry Mulligan was one of its most important exponents, with a number of his solos featured on the *Birth of the Cool* recordings. Mulligan is an important figure in the development of 'cool jazz'. This style is often associated with the West Coast of the United States, where Mulligan was based in the 1950s. He formed a successful quartet with trumpeter Chet Baker in Los Angeles. In 1960 he formed a 13-piece band, recording the album *Concert Jazz Band*.

Mulligan's light, soft tone is typical of cool jazz. He plays in the middle and upper registers, using little vibrato.

His solo is clear and uncomplicated. Mulligan uses a relaxed crotchet and swung quaver movement, and avoids the complex double time of many bebop solos. The melody develops in a logical, unhurried way. He uses silences to create a feeling of space, and each phrase seems to develop organically from the initial idea. For example the melody in the second half of the solo (bars 9–16 in the next example) grows out of the four-note ascending figure that starts at bar 9⁴, with pairs of ascending quavers (marked 'c') repeated higher as the melody ascends.

The accompaniment is for the rhythm section only. The chord pattern is a simpler version of the opening chorus.

At the bridge (section B of Chorus 2) the other frontline instruments enter in quiet low octaves, the C minor tonality darkening the mood. The brighter sound of the trumpet is left out. The frontline melody (still in octaves) climbs quickly to a high F then descends slowly in a sequence of syncopated phrases to a sustained F, two octaves below. The extended descent lengthens this part of the bridge section by two bars (i.e. six bars in total).

Trumpet solo

The trumpet solo begins to the accompaniment of sustained chords in the rest of the ensemble; the bass plays repeated B♭s. After the band's mysterious and meandering descent to the low F during the six preceding bars of section B, the bright sound of the trumpet then transforms the mood. The first four bars of the example that follows are the trumpet solo in B, bringing the return of a regular quaver movement to the melody. There is a clear sense of direction in the modulation through the circle of 5ths and in the way the trumpet melody is shaped. The melody gradually reaches higher and higher until it reaches a top F (bar 4⁴ in the example) – two octaves above the band's low F from four bars earlier.

In the 28 bars led by the trumpet (between Chorus 2 and 3) the role of the accompaniment changes several times; this creates a subtle interplay between Davis and the band. The table below traces the development:

	Trumpet	Other frontline	Rhythm section
End of Chorus 2			
4 bars	Solo melody (notated in trumpet example above) gradually ascends to F	Sustained chords Syncopated chord changes to match ascent of trumpet solo Crescendo	Piano, bass and drums Repeated crotchets in bass: $B\flat m^7 - E\flat^7 -$ $A\flat - D\flat - C^9$
4 bars	Melody part	Full group at climax of trumpet melody Chordal/homophonic; follows rhythm of the melody	Piano drops out Bass and drums only Bass resumes walking pattern
4 bars	Melody	Trumpet, saxophones, trombone in octaves Horn drops out Tuba plays bass Tremolo in baritone sax and tuba on final sustained chord	Bass and drums
Beginning of Chorus 3			
8 bars	Improvised solo A bar of double time	Chords, antiphonal Crushed note (acciaccatura) and falling 3rd figure Fall-off on last chord	Piano, bass and drums Detached chords in piano
8 bars	Improvised solo Use of silences/rests	No other frontline players	Rhythm section only

Chorus 3

The table above covers Section A of Chorus 3 (and the trumpet solo). At Section B, the bridge, the texture is reduced to that of a jazz piano trio. John Lewis' eight-bar piano solo continues the consistent pattern of the solos so far; he uses a relaxed swung quaver movement and a long silence between the phrases. The first four bars of his melody emphasise the interval of a perfect 5th (B$\flat$ to F). This figure is briefly echoed two octaves lower in the B to F$\sharp$ that starts the second four-bar phrase of Section B.

The piece ends with a full-band reprise of the final A section. There is no coda. Instead, this version of the A section is one bar longer than usual. The ascending 3rd figure over the dominant pedal (referred to as 'b' in the music example on page 146) is now played twice more to extend the melody to a suitable conclusion. The additional syncopated accents in drums and cymbals give the final section an extra sense of swing. The quiet and contained mood continues to the end.

The final three chords – fully scored, but *piano* – repeat the opening three chords of *Boplicity*; they are played in augmentation (longer, sustained notes) with the trumpet ending on a D (6th degree in F major) instead of a C. The drums have a quiet fill on the final chord. The tuba plays a tremolo between two notes before coming to rest on its sonorous low F.

Exercise 39

1. What is cool jazz? How is it different from bebop?

2. Why do you think *Boplicity* interested musicians and critics more than the public when it was first released?

3. Compare the arranging techniques of Duke Ellington and Gil Evans.

4. List the similarities and differences between the trumpet styles of Louis Armstrong and Miles Davis.

5. How did the life of a jazz musician change between the 1920s and the end of the 1940s?

Further reading

Miles Davis – Birth of the Cool: scores from the original parts (including *Boplicity*). Published by Hal Leonard, ISBN 0-634-00682-7.

Miles Davis: The Definitive Biography by Ian Carr. Harper Collins, 1982/1999, ISBN 978-0-006530-26-8. An absorbing account of Davis' life and music, including his classic album *A Kind of Blue*, his collaborations with Gil Evans and his later experiments with jazz-rock fusion.

It's About That Time: Miles Davis on and off the record by Richard Cook. Atlantic Books, 2005, ISBN 978-1-84354-332-9. An insightful guide to Davis' many recorded albums.

Gil Evans: Out of the Cool – his life and music by Stephanie Stein Crease. A Cappella Books, Chicago, 2002, ISBN 978-1-556529-85-6. A readable and appreciative account of Gil Evans and his achievements.

Questions on the jazz recordings

In Section B of the listening paper you will hear an extract from one of the three jazz recordings you have studied. You will be expected to be able to recognise which part of the complete recording it comes from and to answer a short series of questions worth 15 marks. These might ask you about:

➤ Who the performers are

➤ The performing techniques that they are using (such as the use of a mute or glissandi)

➤ When and where the recording was made.

Or you may be asked:

➤ To describe the music of a particular passage (such as the accompaniment or the use of a motif)

➤ To compare the chorus or a solo improvisation with one from elsewhere in the whole recording.

In Section C of the paper, which we look at in more detail in the next chapter, you might be asked:

➢ To compare the jazz styles used in two of the recordings you have studied

➢ To compare the role of an instrument in one of the three jazz recordings with the way a composer scored it in one of the three orchestral scores

➢ To place one of the jazz recordings in a historical context, or to compare its background with that of another jazz recording or orchestral score.

Section C questions

For Section C of the paper you will have to write an essay – the only long piece of writing that you are asked to do for AS Music. You should take care over how you structure and express your answer because your quality of language will also be assessed.

You will have to answer **one** question from a choice of three. The questions will give you the opportunity to focus more closely on one or two of the six pieces you will have studied, but don't bank on your favourites coming up – you will have to be ready to write about any of them. Some questions might ask for a comparison between two of the pieces, perhaps about techniques of handling instruments, others might explore your knowledge of the context of one of them (explained below), or you may be asked about issues to do with reception, transmission or performance practice.

The better you know the music, the more convincing your answer is likely to be. Each time you make a general remark, such as how an instrument is used, you will make more of an impression on the examiner if you refer to precise examples from the piece concerned.

Your essay must answer the question set – irrelevant material, even if correct, is unlikely to receive credit. For example, if the question asks about Vivaldi's writing for strings, you will only waste time if you start by outlining the composer's life and works, or if you discuss other matters, such as form or tonality. Try to answer concisely and remember that you won't get marks for repeating points you have already made.

Context

You will be expected to have developed a 'contextual awareness', that is an understanding of the broad background to the orchestral scores and jazz recordings that you have been studying; and your knowledge of any specific details that are known about the genesis of each piece – in other words, how it came into being. You need to know when and where the music was composed or first heard, and what sort of occasion it was for. For some pieces, little detail may be known, in which case you may have to focus on what concerts or recordings were usually like at the time.

Try to form a rough picture in your mind of places, types of building (venue) and audiences. What sort of people were they? Why had they come and what did they expect? Who were the musicians? How did they earn a living?

After closely studying the six pieces you should know quite a lot about the instruments and the ensembles involved. Compare the sort of orchestra used in Beethoven's Violin Concerto with Ellington's band for *Koko*. How similar or different are the instruments and the ways in which they are combined? How has technology changed the sound that they make? How do the performing techniques differ?

Essay-writing

The practice questions below will give you a good idea of the sort of essay you will be asked to write in the exam. Jot down half-a-dozen points about each of them as they occur to you and then practise your essay-writing technique by developing your notes into full answers for at least two of them. Remember that the way you express yourself and present your ideas will be assessed, so it is important to aim to be coherent and clear in the way you use words and shape sentences. Be careful about spelling: if you misspell the names of musicians or titles of pieces it will give a bad impression to the examiner.

Although there is a lot to do in the time, don't rush to spill everything you know about a particular piece down on the paper: take a few moments to think carefully about what the question is asking: what does the question expect you to do? Is it to compare, to describe, or to explain? Which pieces? How many of them? Which aspects? Make sure that what you write is really relevant: don't go into details of how bassoons are constructed if the question is about improvising techniques. Above all, the examiner wants to know how well you really know the music. The most convincing way to show this is by referring to an example – a melody, a riff, a chord, a rimshot – to illustrate the point in your answer. Be as precise as you can: explain exactly where in the music your example occurs, for instance 'the first trumpet riff can be heard at the start of the second chorus'.

Practice questions

1. Discuss the principal differences between the orchestras of Vivaldi and Beethoven, and how the composers wrote for them.

2. Explain the circumstances in which **either** Haydn composed the Symphony No. 103 in E♭ major **or** Beethoven composed the Violin Concerto in D major.

3. If you were asked to prepare a performance of one of the prescribed orchestral works, what aspects would you need to consider? To what extent do you think it is important to respect the composer's intentions?

4. Compare the way music was made available to audiences during 1920–1960 with the customs during the 18th and early 19th centuries. Refer in your answer to the background of one of the orchestral scores and one of the jazz recordings that you have studied.

5. What similarities and differences were there between the working conditions of orchestral players in the 18th and early 19th centuries, compared to the jazz musicians in 1920–1960?

6. Compare the contributions of Louis Armstrong and Miles Davis to the jazz recordings you have studied.

7. Explain which musical features of **either** Charlie Parker's *Ko-ko* **or** Duke Ellington's *Koko* would have been familiar to audiences of the 1940s and which features would have been new.

8. Describe the effect of radio and recording on the work of jazz musicians. Consider issues such as the advance of technology, the role of the radio and recording companies, the artistic and business opportunities presented by radio and recording, and the public response to broadcast and recorded performances.

9. Compare how Haydn or Beethoven used woodwind and brass instruments with the use of reeds and brass in one of the prescribed jazz recordings.

Further reading

You will probably have some favourites among the works you have been studying and might like to find out more about them. Or you may be asking some questions of your own – how was an early bassoon made? How were early microphones different from those in use today? How did jazz spread beyond America? How is vibrato produced on a violin?

Depending on what you want to know, you may find the resources listed below helpful. The ultimate reference work for musicians is *The New Grove Dictionary of Music and Musicians* edited by Stanley Sadie and John Tyrrell (Oxford University Press, 2004, ISBN 978-0-195170-67-9). There is a separate *New Grove Dictionary of Jazz* by Barry Kernfeld (Oxford University Press, 2003, ISBN 978-1-561 592-84-5). Most major libraries have a reference copy and some allow borrowers to access the online version free of charge. However, it is extremely detailed and you may find that it tells you so much that it is difficult to get all the information straight in your head. The *Cambridge Music Guide* edited by Stanley Sadie and Alison Latham (Cambridge University Press, 1990, ISBN 978-0- 521399-42-5) is a useful and more manageable resource.

Internet sites

There is a wealth of information available on the internet, but remember that standards of accuracy and reliability vary. If you are a regular user of Wikipedia you will already know that while it is often a good starting point for research, the information there is not always correct in every detail. Some record companies put the sleeve notes from CDs on their websites and these can be a useful source of additional information.

Do remember that many music websites focus on biographical information about musicians, which will often not be relevant to your course. Try to use the web to answer questions about the music itself. Focus on the areas of study and building up your technical knowledge about the music you are studying.

The BBC Radio 3 website has useful information on both classical music and jazz. You can also listen to recent broadcasts online and follow links to other useful sites.

Recordings

It is advisable to study more than one recording of each of the set orchestral scores. For the set jazz repertoire it is essential to study the precise recordings listed on page 70. Don't forget that radio and TV are free sources of music: search the listings weekly, including channels that you don't normally turn to.

Index

Acknowledgements

The authors would like to thank the consultant Sally Ellerington and the editorial and design team of Harriet Power, Katharine Allenby and Christina Forde. The authors and publisher are grateful to the following publishers for permission to use printed excerpts from their publications:

The Pink Panther Theme. Music by Henry Mancini. © Copyright 1964 Northridge Music Co. and EMI U Catalog Inc., USA. All Rights Reserved. International Copyright Secured.

Alligator Crawl. Words & Music by Thomas 'Fats' Waller. © Copyright 1918 Redwood Music Limited. All Rights Reserved. International Copyright Secured.

Ko Ko. Words & Music by Charlie Parker. © Copyright 1945 Savoy Music Company, USA. Screen Gems-EMI Music Limited. All Rights Reserved. International Copyright Secured.

Cherokee. Words & Music by Ray Noble. © Copyright 1938 Redwood Music Limited. All Rights Reserved. International Copyright Secured.

It Ain't Necessarily So (From *Porgy And Bess*). Music by George Gershwin. © Copyright 2011 Dorsey Brothers Music Limited. All Rights Reserved. International Copyright Secured.

Hotter Than That. Music by Lillian Hardin. © Copyright 1928 Leeds Music Corporation, USA. Universal/MCA Music Limited. All rights in Germany administered by Universal/MCA Music Publ. GmbH. All Rights Reserved. International Copyright Secured.

Ko Ko. Words & Music by Duke Ellington. © Copyright Robbins Music Corporation, USA. EMI United Partnership Limited. All Rights Reserved. International Copyright Secured.

Boplicity (Be Bop Lives). Words & Music by Miles Davis & Gil Evans. © Copyright 1949 Jazz Horn Music Corporation, USA. Universal/MCA Music Limited (50%)(All rights in Germany administered by Universal/MCA Music Publ. GmbH)/Copyright Control (50%). All Rights Reserved. International Copyright Secured.